# TEACHING

*in the same series*
*Architecture* J. M. Richards

*in preparation*
*Banking* Evan Hughes
*Medicine* Jane Gray

THE PROFESSIONS

# TEACHING

John Watts

DAVID & CHARLES
NEWTON ABBOT LONDON
NORTH POMFRET (VT) VANCOUVER

ISBN 0 7153 6481 2

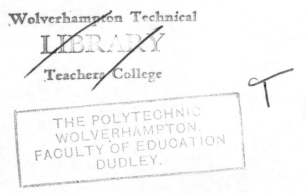
Set in 11 on 13pt Garamond and printed in
Great Britain by Latimer Trend & Company Ltd Plymouth
for David & Charles (Holdings) Limited
South Devon House Newton Abbot Devon

Published in the United States of America
by David & Charles Inc North Pomfret
Vermont 05053 USA

Published in Canada by Douglas David &
Charles Limited 3645 McKechnie Drive
West Vancouver BC

# Contents

To Liz, my wife, for keeping the balance

# Introduction

Many worthy books on education appear each month. The specialist needs to read furiously to keep up with them, let alone do anything about them. Why another one? Mainly to say something to those outside the education trade about what it means and feels like to be in it. Inside, we are a contentious lot, divided, and argumentative, practitioners pitted against theorists, progressives battling against traditionalists. But from outside we must appear much of a muchness, just as do 'the medical profession' or 'the trade unions'. What I have tried to do is to open us up for view somewhat, to differentiate and point out variety.

Naturally, I cannot speak for the whole teaching profession. (Ten organisations exist for teachers in schools and colleges of further education, with 300,000 members.) Collectively, we do not yet have one voice, and I would not presume to anticipate it. I can only speak of what I know. Teachers work in such varied fields, their pupils including such diversity as handicapped infants and graduate biochemists. Some areas of this world I know of only at second-hand, and may draw only on the reports of others. Some areas remain as unexplored foreign parts to me: I know nothing about teaching in, say, approved schools or polytechnics, and consequently I have neglected them. The true source of this book is my own direct experience, what I have seen, heard, smelled, touched and tasted for myself.

As everyone has been to school, so everyone feels qualified to comment on education. I wouldn't mind having a pound for every time I have heard a parent say 'I don't hold with educational theories and all that nonsense', and then had to listen to them expounding their own strongly expressed and highly idiosyncratic theory of education. It does not make for good parent-teacher relationships to tell each of these that what I have heard is a biased and ill-founded medley of dogmatic opinion and limited experience, but I often say that to explain my position after twenty years in the business I should need to write them a book. Well, here it is.

Of course, teachers are themselves notorious for resting their cases on opinion and experience. This is not enough. We all need to study the findings of other people's research instead of indulging in the easy laugh about the tendency of researchers to spend time and money coming up with the answers we all knew in the first place. They sometimes do, in which case they substantiate our hunches (bully for us!), but as often as not they cause us to modify our opinion, whether we acknowledge it or not. (For instance, anyone of the opinion that large sums of money should be spent in discouraging fifteen-year-olds from smoking, will eventually be affected by the research finding that most fifteen-year-old smokers had formed the habit by the age of eleven.)

So what I have to say is a blend of recollected experience, study-based theory, and plain hunch. It arises from those years in the classroom with a very wide cross section of our secondary school population, a period in teacher training, an acquaintanceship with research and the added perspectives of headship. I have tried to convey something of how it has been to live as a teacher, to paint a picture of a landscape with variegated figures but, true to my kind, however critical I am of our tendency to preach, I have prescribed as well as described.

There is one apology I should like to give in advance. Wherever I have written 'him' for the teacher, you should read 'him and/or her'. The defect does not derive from any unrealised male chauvinism on my part but solely from a total inability to overcome the problem stylistically.

Countesthorpe, 1974                                    JOHN WATTS

CHAPTER ONE

# Who Wants to Teach?

An indignant senior mistress said to me, in the year of the first Sputnik, 'That boy Morris in your form just told me that he wanted to become a doctor on a spaceship. Twelve years old, and no more realistic ambition than that—I don't know what rubbish their heads will get filled with next!' Perhaps a Youth Employment Officer straightened him out later, I don't know. All I do know is that at his age my ambition was to take a boat to West Africa, make my way into the jungle and live among the apes. But then I was an avid reader of Edgar Rice Burroughs.

At seventeen I thought I was going to be an engineer, which in my case was scarcely more realistic than becoming Tarzan. I had been put on to advanced science in the sixth form because I had done marginally better in that subject than in the others at School Certificate, and that was because the subject had novelty value for me, unlike French, say, or History. It was a curious Science Sixth. From it emerged one able gynaecologist, one brilliant painter, now a restaurateur of distinction, a failed actor, and one of the world's most brilliant writers of science-fiction. And me—who had no notion then of ever becoming a teacher, or taking a degree in Philosophy and English Literature, or writing a book like this.

When I come to think of it, I can recall no more than one or two schoolboys who ever indicated an ambition to teach, and in each of their cases it was to become a teacher of Physical Education, in other words, to remain pretty firmly outside any classroom. With girls the picture is rather different. Much more frequently I have found that they would like to be teachers, and their parents have approved of this because it offered prospects of a finishing school at a training college or university, followed by a respectable and secure occupation until marriage, or beyond it, or without it. They were almost always the most industrious, obedient and priggish girls: never those madcaps who truanted, joined in subversive activities, got through dozens of boy friends, or argued defiantly with their elders and betters. When selecting applicants for teacher training at the London Institute of Education, I found myself strenuously resisting those coming forward for the next stage in their head-girl syndrome.

The truth is that very few of us knew at the age of sixteen what we would be doing at twenty-six, or thirty-six. I suspect that men and women in most occupations would be hard put to it to explain their position as the end of a logical sequence of carefully weighed decisions. Some do. I once had in one class of thirty eleven-year-olds a girl whose ambition was to become a nurse and a boy who knew he was going to be a doctor. Both have since done exactly that. They were rare exceptions in unusually high proportion. Of the others in that class, one is a car mechanic, which was not entirely unpredictable as his father owned a garage, and one is an established concert contralto, which no one could have foreseen.

So what brings anyone into teaching? How did I, as a case in point, reach the front of the classroom? I think it started when as a very unmotivated subaltern in Germany the year after the war ended, I saw children starving and was told to take no notice as it was their fault for bombing Coventry and they needed to learn a lesson. Perhaps they weren't starving, but only undernourished, and perhaps bony kids had always rummaged through the garbage bins behind the officers' clubs, and certainly not so many of those I saw then have died since as perished the year before in Dresden, or possibly a little before that in London and Coventry. But I didn't reason like that at the time: I only saw future hope being blighted by past hatreds, and that these children, many without homes and parents, were the only ones who could build anything better upon the old ruins. You might argue that this should have intensified ambitions to be an engineer and precipitated me into the building industry. I know that for some of my friends at the time it did just that, and I could point to splendid buildings (some of them schools) and dams and roadways they have built. But for me it had to be people. And as I look back now I find that dangerously presumptuous.

Dangerous because it assumed that I was hoping to shape people, as my friends would go on more humbly to shape concrete, steel and timber. Didn't Hitler as well as Dr Arnold shape people? In what image was I going to shape them? By what *Fuhrerprinzip* would I educate them? I wasn't all that sure of any models at that time of low ebb, and years of boredom on cricket field and in chapel had made me sceptical of 'character training'. All I was sure of, as the first atomic fall-out settled and the Nuremberg trials opened, was that I could hardly do worse for the second half of the century than had been done by others for the first. I have long since accepted that Education does not change the world, of which more later, but I believe that many have entered teaching in order to do just that.

There were counter-pressures, giving me good reasons for not taking up teaching. For one thing, the army, until I got overseas, seemed to be made up evenly of recruits, old sweats, and instructors. Instructors made sure we knew all we needed to know, from how to slope arms to how to blow up a bridge. The instructors pushed and pulled us about like so much plasticine. They made things happen to us without ever knowing us: they conditioned our reflexes but denied our existence. If I really learnt anything from them, I learnt to survive. We were even instructed, during officer training, in how to instruct. At this stage I could detect which of the training officers were schoolmasters. Not the ones who said things like 'Look you chaps, you've got to know what the procedures are for a court martial, so we've just got to dredge into this huge dreary volume of the King's Regulations, all right?' No, the schoolmasters were the ones who seemed utterly convinced that the King's Regulations, or whatever buff-coloured manual we were to study, was the most fascinating subject which could at that time have fallen into our hands. It could be divided into easy parts, analysed on a board with coloured chalks, be summarised, dramatised, or provide the material for lecturettes. How I remember those lecturettes. I once had to give a ten-minute lecturette on 'The Use of Visual Aids'. When I had filled in my time, the instructor leapt in gleefully, like a Jack Russell terrier being introduced to a fox-hole. 'Yes,' he shrilled (all these instructors in instruction were shrill and staccato). 'Yes. But what has he forgotten? The one obvious thing to include and he's left it out. What is it?' One sleepy traitor, with a sly and self-exculpating grin at me, raises a hand. (Someone has to provide The Right Answer to show we are thinking things out for ourselves.) 'What is it he's left out? Yes. Of course. He's not illustrated his lecturette with a single Visual Aid.'

The schoolmaster instructors were the ones who knew that you had to Make the Subject Interesting. Since this implied that of itself the subject was *un*interesting, everything depended on their performance or, as they would prefer to call it, their technique. 'There is technique for teaching anything,' one of them told me, 'even how to darn a sock or peel a potato.' If I became a teacher, would I have to become a performer like that? Or could I rely on at least having a subject that interested me, no, more than that, that concerned me as a whole being? Socks! Potatoes! Yet I am still finding children set tasks like writing up their dictated notes on How to Polish a Pair of Shoes, or an essay on How to Mend a Puncture.

Still, with all these dreadful warnings, I applied to train as a teacher. I only then realised that there were two ways to qualify

14

to teach and that these represented an enormous division. It is a division related directly to the division into Disraeli's 'two nations'. None of those immediate post-war aspirations did more than blur that division; the 1944 Education Act by establishing a category of secondary modern schools only tried to make it nicer than it had been on the wrong side of the divide, and the development more recently of comprehensive schooling to bridge that divide, has not been accompanied by any comparable reform in the training of teachers.

I had never been inside a school other than my own and those against whom we played rugby. I knew from my parents before the war that there were council schools, hidden away from sight somewhere, presumably on council estates, but they were nothing to do with us. The one couple amongst my parents' circle who sent their son to the council school were considered to be irresponsible and unloving, facts borne out by poor little Jimmy's appalling cockney accent and uncouth manners. As his parents played golf, we were allowed to have contact with Jimmy, and his defects were only discussed discreetly, as if he were mongoloid, or someone from a far-away country with an incomprehensible culture, odd but tolerable in one representative, but not to be encouraged in any greater numbers.

It began to dawn on me at this time that schoolteachers trained to teach in council schools, but schoolmasters, and presumably schoolmistresses were born, so the legend ran, not trained, read for degrees at Oxford or Cambridge, and then infected their pupils at selective schools with a love of their subject. Furthermore, schoolteachers instructed their pupils in how to take instruction, show respect for authority, earn an honest penny and take it all with a grin. Schoolmasters, on the other hand, formed the character of future leaders, teaching them to submit to discipline in the knowledge that they in turn would then be able to administer it. It was the army all over again. Instructors and recruits, some to become officers, the rest other ranks. Certainly, I didn't want to become either, being now deeply suspicious of those displaying or busily acquiring what were called the 'qualities of leadership'. Was there no escape? Was it only a future of either one or the other? Perhaps it could be changed. It seemed, at least, something worth fighting for.

I wrote to the University of Oxford before I discovered that there isn't actually any such place. I found out about Wardens and Provosts and Masters and wrote to them all from my dark corner in Germany. In the end I found that if I could add Latin to my School Certificate, I could be admitted to the Faculty of Arts at Bristol University to study over three years for the degree of Bachelor of Arts in English.

I was now a civilian, under orders from nobody for the first time in my life, so it was of my own free will that I studied Latin and took a temporary teaching job. I took nine months to move from '*mensa*, a table' to Ovid's *Metamorphoses* and Caesar's *Gallic Wars*, taking a weekly lesson from a friend in exchange for baby-sitting. For most of that time I earned a living of sorts teaching English to foreigners, either at home in my room over the greengrocers in the Fulham Road, or at the Berlitz School in Oxford Street. This is a side-line form of teaching in the network that this book tries to cover, but still each year foreigners flock to England and learn our tongue at a large number of tutorial schools, with particular clusters in London and Cambridge. Some of the conditions will have changed over the last twenty-five years, but I doubt if it is basically any different, so it may be worth a glimpse into that ant-hill as it was.

The essence of Berlitz teaching was that only the language to be learnt was used in the lessons, which meant that I could teach students of any nationality. They mostly came singly but sometimes, when at the same standard, in pairs, like the old Polish couple stumbling painfully over and over the first sentences, so anxious to please, or the Norwegian mother and daughter who bobbed up and down in their seats in rhythm with their sing-song intonation. We sat in little cells, just large enough for the desk between us. I became adept at reading print upside down.

I taught nationals of over twenty different countries and soon differentiated the various quirks of our language that held them up, amusing or infuriating them. I remember an energetic French businessman who insisted on starting every lesson by gasping out 'Arry where's your 'at? It's 'anging on the 'anger in the 'all.' It never improved. There was a meek Swiss girl who wrote me the story of how her father had trained her to become the champion rifle-shot of her town. Her landlady wasn't feeding her too well, it seemed, so she used to visit the hen-run down her garden every day and eat a few raw eggs. I advised her to shoot rabbits. Food was still rationed then. But my favourite was a big ponderous Chinaman who asked my advice about packing parcels. A friend in Kent was sending him eggs by post and whenever he opened up the wrappings it turned out that, as he picturegrammed it for me, 'The eggs they break and they vomit.' He taught me patience.

The Berlitz School is irrelevant to our educational system, but I learnt one thing there that was fundamental to my becoming a teacher. This was that if one was not going to be an instructor, then one could not teach a subject but only teach people. It had proved impossible to teach English to my foreign students without becoming intrigued by each one's individual concerns and interests. They learnt whatever English they did from me as an outcome of establishing a relationship with me. The school forbade us to engage in discussion of sex, religion or politics, which may not leave much of interest, yet even with such topics as packaging eggs or marksmanship, it was possible to let the learning take place through the exchange of personal concern. Of language it was certainly true to say that it only made sense when understood to be an expression of human relationship involving both the speaker and the listener, writer and the reader; it could never be regarded as something external to the user, could not be conveyed as something objective, a commodity, like a coat or a hat, however well made to measure. I felt that some teachers I had already seen could not draw this conclusion, in which case all this expressive chat would appear to them to be a self-indulgent waste of time that should be spent instead on listing idioms or rationalising the idiosyncrasies of English usage into a grammar. There were others, having some inkling of its value, who found themselves personally unable to establish this necessary rapport with their students. I found that I could. Not wanting now to leave teaching in the hands of all these instructors, I determined to press on.

I went to university, took a degree, and in my fourth year stayed in Bristol's Department of Education to take the qualifying certificate. At that time it was sufficient to hold a degree in order to teach, though it has since become necessary for graduates to take the post-graduate certificate in education. So there were four routes into teaching from which I could have chosen in that post-war period. (1) One-year emergency training, a route taken by many ex-servicemen who had been instructors in the armed forces; (2) two years at a teachers' training college, which in the 1960s became Colleges of Education with three-year courses in an attempt to level up the training to university status; (3) three-year degree course at university with direct entry to school-teaching but with no specialist teaching preparation, now regarded as insufficient qualification in the maintained school system; (4) three-year degree course followed by one-year teacher training in a university Department of Education. I deal with training more fully in Chapter 6, and show how the picture today is altered.

Two of the reasons for my own decision to teach I would now reject. I no longer believe the world can be put to rights by merely giving children good education, and I am not so sure now that I can teach any better than most of those who taught me. That is not to say that world changes to the benefit of mankind cannot be prepared for by education; I am sure they can. And I think that I have had many advantages over those who taught me, more opportunity to carry their ideas through, little excuse for not being as effective as them. Nevertheless, two strong incentives for anyone wanting to become a teacher are the belief that by teaching one may contribute to the improvement of mankind's lot, and the desire to work out some of the injustices suffered in one's own schooldays. The two very often go together, in fact.

I have spent many hours in the last three years interviewing graduates, and university students in their final year, who had applied to train as teachers. In some way or other I would ask them the inevitable question 'Why do you want to teach? It's tough work, exhausting and often shattering. Why are you choosing this way of earning a living?' Their most common reply was that they wanted to share with the young their love for their subject. Rather cynically, I know that with many this meant that they enjoyed undergraduate study, were unlikely to stay on for post-graduate research, could not face a complete break and wanted to remain as near as possible to the academic life.

Now a love of a subject studied to a high level is admirable, though it can, not only in subjects as remote as Egyptology or Old Norse, be a handicap in planning a curriculum that is appropriate to our present-day schools. Someone recently out of university with a passion for Biochemistry or French Literature is invaluable in a sixth form, passing this enthusiasm to those who, with a little inspiration of this sort, will shortly become undergraduates themselves. But it is quite inadequate for teaching at anything below sixth form; in fact it may well cause an impatience with those whose interests are likely still to be very diverse, and a scorn for those who clearly are not going to adopt the particular golden specialism of their teacher. Equally, to enter teaching because you don't want to leave the happy land of student life, whether to you it offers the tranquil groves of academe or the field of personal and political expression free from the social constraints of earning an income, smacks too much of delayed adolescence to stand as a valid reason for facing the hard realities of schools other than the most sheltered of selective colleges.

On the other hand, to be effective, a teacher really does need to feel that there is worth in helping a pupil to solve quadratic equations, or master the German syntax, that the pupil will through his agency have added something of value to his own competence. It is a question of priority. Does your subject exist in its own right, to be cherished and passed down from the select to the select? Or is it one of the means by which your pupils are going to learn about themselves and the world, just as did those who developed the subject? A supplementary question that I would put to those who want to teach from love of their subject is 'Could you envisage your subject undergoing any modification as a result of your introducing schoolchildren to it?' If the answer to that is Yes, as has certainly been the case in the teaching of my own subject, then love of subject, not as a cherished, immutable body of erudition, but as an extrusion, an outcome of interactions between individuals, others, and the external world, may be a perfectly acceptable reason for anyone wanting to teach.

One has somehow to find out the answer to the question posed by that committee lady in the floral hat, 'Do you like children?' (In interview one looks for subtler ways of finding this out, not always successfully; quite recently I winced to hear a colleague on an interviewing panel put that self-same question, then saw the applicant, an obviously brilliant ceramic artist, think carefully and reply 'No, I honestly can't say I do.' She had only then realised that her dedication was to her craft, her subject, and not to teaching schoolchildren.) The question is crucial. If you find neither amusement nor pleasure in the ways of growing boys and girls, their kingfisher changes of mood, their predictable jokes, their try-ons and goadings, their group fads, the individual enthusiasms that they ask you to share, then teaching is a killer, psychological and physical. They don't want to be patronised, and they can see through phoney mateyness at a glance, tearing it to shreds at half a chance, but they want to know, and they can size this up in a trice, whether you are for them or not.

The other most frequent reason given by students for wanting to teach is the desire to give school pupils a fairer deal. This desire to see justice done by kids is replacing the older hope of putting the world to rights, and seems to me to be more practicable. It places the concern with the present rather than the future. It is horrifying to discover how many people remember their school-days with a sense of injustice. I myself often felt in my army days that military justice, though hard, was fair in a way that school justice had seldom been. The adult has such an immediate and obvious advantage over the child that he needs to pay scant regard to the laws of evidence, and needs to refer to no objective scale of punishments and to fear no court of higher appeal. With such little restraint, it is no wonder that teachers have often abused their power. The abuse is seldom brought to public notice until a generation later, which only allows that sense of injustice to fester. Humiliation, very often achieved by sarcasm, has been the teachers' staple weapon, one more in need of abolition than the cane, be-cause its scars are so much more lasting, and a weapon more likely to be used on a sensitive and able child than the cane. I always liked to start a course with students in training by asking them to put themselves back in the child's position and recall their earliest school memories. It was here that I discovered how many of them were taking up teaching in order to redress the grievances they themselves had suffered. They unmistakably wanted to change, not the whole social fabric, but the way children were taught in schools.

Of course, these are the initial attractions for the new entrant. What satisfactions may there be for the established teacher? For a start, he may continue to enjoy seeing his pupils respond to his subject, and he may take pride in the development of their personalities without having to inflict injustices upon them: in other words, there is no reason why the initial attractions should fade with time. But he may experience satisfactions over and above these.

The teacher has as many frustrations from officialdom as most other people earning a living, he suffers 'the Law's delay, the insolence of office'. But taking that into account, the British teacher enjoys great freedom in the manner in which he teaches. He may be required to conform over extraneous matters such as the marking of registers or the timing of reports to parents, but there is enormous freedom in the choice and development of one's own style of teaching. I will raise later in the book the question of how far new developments in schools, laudable as they may be, are modifying this freedom, but as yet the situation has altered little. As long as a teacher in his classroom is not disturbing his neighbouring colleagues, and provided he leaves things in recognisable shape for whoever uses his room after him, he can virtually do as he likes with his class. He may arrange his desks in rows facing him, he may arrange them in dispersed knots; he may deliver monologues, or he may, to establish a major point about language, refuse for weeks on end to say a single word, communicating only in writing; he may employ a whole arsenal of audio-visual aids, or he may be remembered, because he sings Yorkshire folk-songs to his class. He may be pressed by an eager head of department or a dominant head but, by and large, if his pupils tolerate him and results are not disastrous, the hierarchy will leave him alone. Most heads still rather like writing *and* reading confidentials that say 'Mister So-and-So's methods may be idiosyncratic, verging at times even on eccentricity, but there is no denying that . . .' etc, etc. And if the head objects or advisers advise, the teacher who is resolute in his own conviction as to what he is doing has little to fear as there is no contractual requirement as to *how* he teaches. This has its negative side too, as I shall point out later, but for someone who values an independent mode of working, teaching is a secure base.

There are other ways in which teaching offers security, though these too in turn create problems in the schools. Once qualified, a teacher needs to complete a probationary year in full employment and if his reports are then satisfactory and his appointment confirmed he enjoys security of tenure. It is virtually impossible for him to be dismissed except on grounds of negligence or immorality. At the lowest level this means that he has only to be careful to carry straight on until retirement and a pension. At the best it enables a teacher to concentrate on work and the long-term development of his effectiveness, or career, without the fear of capricious dismissal or threat of redundancy. Although teaching lagged behind other professions in provision for widows and orphans, that too is covered by the scheme introduced in 1967.

Of course, no one likes to say so, but one attraction to teaching is the extensive paid holiday time. Schools are normally open for 190 days in a year. On a five-day-week basis, most people work more like 250 days in a year, which leaves the teacher with the equivalent of two months additional time off. True, a teacher needs time out of school, released from pupil contact, to keep up with reading, writing, preparation of materials, to go on courses and conferences, to talk with other teachers, to think. Some give a lot of their time to these activities, some regularly take parties of schoolchildren away with them, and that's no holiday; others travel alone to refresh their subject, whether it is Homer or Home Economics. But, let's face it, for most of us it is the biggest bonus in a job with next to no perquisites. As a young teacher I used to be defensive about jibes from friends, and others not so friendly, who commented resentfully on my free time. I would tot up for them the hours that I spent on mapping out new courses for my pupils, arguing that you needed to renew your material continuously if it was not to become stale and dated very quickly, and I would rehearse the titles of books, articles and periodicals that I needed to read just to keep abreast, for one has to be a student for as long as you are a teacher. And so on. All of it perfectly true. Nowadays though, I just say to any challenger that, yes, I do have nice long holidays, have had time to be with my family as they grew up, or to get on with doing things that I want to do, and wouldn't you just like to be a teacher!

Well, would any of them like to be a teacher? Many people might think better of it when they contemplate what they might end up like as a person. 'I wouldn't like to become like the typical teacher,' they say. And well they might if the stereotype is of someone rather 'loud-voiced, somewhat pompous, decidedly dogmatic, fond of telling people where they are wrong, very fussy about trifles, and quite certain that nobody would ever take him for a teacher'.* An unsympathetic portrait; but the characteristics, though changing, and almost totally absent in those who have taken up teaching in the last five years, are unfortunately all too familiar.

If any of us appear like that we have only ourselves to blame ultimately, but to a large extent this 'typical teacher' is the creature of a society demanding a certain kind of teaching. For centuries the teacher has been allotted a custodian's function, has needed to become 'skilled to rule', and this has given him too frequently his loud voice (or her shrill one). He has been required to combine these sergeant-major skills with the power to express the moral authority of a priest, so it is hardly surprising if he becomes pompous and fond of telling people where they are wrong. While expecting to embody this moral authority he found little of the world's grosser immoralities, slavery, corruption, extortion, in his school room, so that his darts of fiery indignation had to be hurled at such petty transgressions as spelling mistakes, nose-picking and infringements of clothing regulations. Above all, as long as teaching is seen as the transference of knowledge from the informed teacher to the ignorant pupil, so there will be an enormous emphasis on right answers, the teacher knowing them and the pupil learning to give them. The teacher, in this role, cannot admit to error or ignorance without loss of face, and the pupil can enjoy playing the game of catching him out. No wonder that the teacher became habitually defensive and self-righteous,

* G. L. Lamb, *Questions Answered about Teaching* (1949)

so that 'e'en though vanquished, he could argue still'. And in the isolation of his classroom, concentrating on what he wanted his pupils to be like, he lacked the opportunity, open to other adults in daily concourse with others, of seeing himself as others saw him, and in the absence of a realistic self-image then believed that outside the school nobody would take him for a teacher.

It is still going on, but it is changing. Steadily, as I hope to make clearer in the following chapter, the concepts of teaching and learning have altered. As the teacher becomes less authoritarian, either because he learns that he can't win that way, or because he wishes his pupils to become co-operative rather than submissive, so he becomes less hectoring. As the pupils are increasingly taught to find out for themselves, exploring and investigating *with* the teacher, rather than remaining dependent on the teacher for the right answer, so the teacher becomes less inclined to keep correcting others, more tolerant of ambiguity, more open to speculation. He becomes a person in his own right, lives outside his syllabus much more, is known to share interests with his pupils and, therefore, is less inclined to be pompous. And with the emergence of a pluralistic society, the teacher is less likely to be used as a model for a single set of class mores, expected, like the priest, to exemplify a standard of conduct not required of others, who are only human after all. He, and even more, she, is no longer that paragon of middle-class virtue, never seen with a pint pot in hand or eating fish and chips out of a newspaper or wearing a shirt without a tie. Less of a prig and more of a neighbour.

All of this may render us more ordinary, and in so doing may it not demand as its price loss of respect and of self-respect? This raises the issue of the teacher in society, which I shall return to later. In a society stratified by incomes, according to the Registrar-General's model, teachers, like priests, have for long been given a deference out of keeping with their salaries. The respect was, however, mingled with fear and contempt. It was a respect grounded in submission to strength of will and arm, in recognition of superior knowledge; it was a lasting respect because it was acquired during the formative years of childhood but grudged because there remained no power to back the authority later. As a headmaster I met many parents on their first visit to me stammering in fear and resentment, under self-imposed formality, quite evidently regressing to the last time they were before the head, cowed and humiliated. Later they would tell me how their old head kept his cane on his desk and 'My word, we respected that! He didn't need to tell us twice.'

Well, that's one kind of respect. Increasingly now we hope for a different kind, if we are to receive any at all. We may in time come to feel the respect of our neighbours because we can identify the problems of their children, learning problems and behaviour problems, because we have tried to help them overcome them, because we have given our time and expertise to them without clocking up the hours of our availability. This respect may be the greater if at the same time we are not visitors from another world, but share problems of living with those whose children we teach. And the self-respect that may grow from this also derives from the teacher's knowledge that he is not exploiting these children, not having to regard them as units of population, potential buyers or potential competitors. He is, of course, under pressure to regard them as commodities and to step up his production of Grammar places, Grade One 'O' levels or Open Scholarships, but he can resist.

However, I don't want to replace one stereotype with another, and before I make the new teacher seem merely a cut-price paragon, let us consider something of the variety within teaching, variety of schools, variety of teachers within them, and the various others with whom teachers work.

# CHAPTER TWO

# People in School

A primary school teacher recently said that you only know what it is like to be a teacher when you recognise the smell of wet Wellies on a Monday morning. Barry Tebb, in his poem 'School Smell' remembers it as:

> Composed of chalk dust,
> Pencil shavings and
> The sharp odour
> Of stale urine;
> It meets me now and then
> Creeping down a creosoted corridor
> Or waiting to be banged
> With the dust from piles of books
> On top of a cupboard.

For me, the smell evocative of my schooldays is a mixture of ink and scrubbed floor boards, but that particular aroma is a thing of the past, now that we have ball-points and acoustic flooring. This generation of schoolchildren will no doubt come up with its own evocations of childhood, but for someone teaching now, the key to any impressions of a school's atmosphere will be found in its staffroom. Whatever the relationship a teacher may establish with the pupils, however much contact there may be with care-takers, parents, advisers and others, his condition of life will be affected mainly by those with whom he shares the staffroom, for that is where he will discover the most abiding community and conflict.

The staffroom will immediately betray the attitudes and relationships of the school, as a community, to any reasonably sensitive newcomer. Just as we tell most about an individual by what he takes for granted, so in the staffroom one can sense what are the priorities and the preoccupations of the teachers because that is where they come to drop their guard and their belongings. A staffroom may resemble the lounge of a private country hotel, where each old lady has her own jealously guarded seat; it may look more like an airport waiting area where people kill time, scan notices and are obviously in transit; there are club-houses and there are coffee-shops; no two are identical.

In all my years as a schoolboy I had never penetrated what was more traditionally called the masters' common room. We exercised our powers of fantasy in speculating what it must be like, building on crumbs of information, such as our French teacher's brief account of how they had to share a sort of Swiss roll known as pink-elephant's trunk for tea. But generally a pupil who ventures to put his head around the staffroom door will be bawled out from inside and traumaticly forget what was seen. So when I was taken as student-on-practice into my first staffroom, at a boys' secondary modern school in Bristol, I can honestly say that I had never seen anything like it.

The room itself might have passed muster as an interrogation cell, with its dingily distempered bare grey walls, windows dimmed by grime and condensation and single bulb hanging under a glass coolie-hat shade from the middle of the ceiling. Beneath this lamp was an enamel-topped table stacked with chipped mugs, piles of dog-eared exercise books, milk bottles, football boots and unidentifiable woollen wear, the whole seemingly sprinkled with granulated sugar. There was a low earthenware sink under the window, and in the far corner stood an antique gas oven. On it a kettle was simmering and out of its black belly a hot pie was being removed by a crouching, cursing figure in a rusty-green track suit. In a great Welsh voice he boomed, 'Make room on the table and keep your hands off my pasty you thieving bastards!' All good-humoured knockabout stuff and an exact indication of life in that school. Probably it was ideal training for below decks in the Merchant Navy, where indeed many of the boys made their way on leaving.

I wouldn't suggest for one moment that this was typical of a secondary modern school. The very next one that I knew was at Sawston where the contrast was total. There were bright curtains to the windows, paintings on the walls, oak tables to work at, shelves of books, flowers from the grounds in vases from the art department, easy chairs, hospitality and some lively conversation. The headmaster joined us there for morning coffee and it was a pleasure to bring a visitor. Of course, it was a mixed staff and the presence of women caused the men to use it as a home, rather than a cross between a rugby club and a university library. If you can imagine such a hybrid, that is how I saw the staffroom of the only boys' grammar school in which I have taught.

What the newcomer will sense most rapidly in a staffroom is the strength of the hierarchy and how far that strength derives from formal position rather than executive competence. If a teacher in a senior post is confident of his ability and knows that those working with him acknowledge this, gain security from him and respect him for it, then he is likely to relax in their company, tending towards an equality of social behaviour. If this seniority is more an expression of age and experience, less likely to be demonstrated by either organising competence, teaching ability or imaginative leadership, then there will be an increased emphasis put upon the formal supports for status. These supports will include formality of manners (do junior members rise to their feet if addressed by a senior member?) rank order in seating on platform, rank order in speaking at staff meetings, extension of privileges by seniority, and so on. An established and conservative school will tend to be status-conscious and status will be conferred from above: a developing and exploratory school will be less status-conscious, more competitive, because status tends to be acquired rather than conferred.

One of the first things a newcomer will want to know in a staffroom is what position others hold, whether in terms of function or rank. (I shall say more in the next chapter about hierarchies and their varieties.) Some people betray themselves at once: there may be the teacher of Physical Education in track-suit with whistle on a braid round the neck, or the Biology mistress with white coat and attendant aroma of formaldehyde. But function may have little to do with the relationships established in staffroom. In a very formal hierarchy the social groupings within staff may depend heavily on age and rank, with the senior master discussing his crossword clues only with heads of major departments, but this is now comparatively rare, and he will more probably discuss them with the young English graduate if he thinks she is more likely to be up on her quotes from Scott or whatever. In other words, the patterns in staffroom probably derive from interests and attitudes rather than rank or function.

Thus there may be a group formed around its daily bridge game. Or another may be made up of women with their own young children, stories of whose misadventures and maladies they can exchange day by day. There will be association by political colour, with fellow *Telegraph* readers having more to say to each other than they would to the *Guardian* readers. Those without family ties may plan their Mediterranean travelling holidays together; more seasoned family men will exchange hints about camping in Wales. There are alliances of sportsmen, of motor mechanics, food-fanatics, environmentalists, transcendentalists: the larger the staff, the greater the variety of interests.

In a healthy staff community these groupings shift, overlap, coalesce, subdivide, rise and fall, with any one member moving in and out of any number of them. Almost inevitably there will be at least one hard-edged, exclusive cell. This can be tolerated in any but the very small staffroom. Something is wrong at a basic level, however, if a majority are confining themselves in permanent cliques. This seems to happen when interests that are not central to the teaching are not overridden by a sense of common purpose there. I have seen it in a hastily reorganised comprehensive school where the staff of the former grammar school isolate themselves from those from the former modern school, each clinging to old sectarian interests or nursing partisan grievances. I have also seen it in the staffroom of a long-established school where any sense of purpose has long been blunted. One of the main responsibilities of a head teacher is to make sure that staff have a common challenge, a shared aim that cuts across the boundaries of any coteries.

When this common purpose is absent, the atmosphere can be very threatening for any new arrival, because he will be isolated from the start. Nicholas Otty, in his revealing account of training and probation, *Learner Teacher*, wrote how 'the staff sit in three irregular but immutable circles in a row down the narrow length of the room. I tend to stand most of the time, but there is a circle to which most of the new staff clearly belong.' He at least had somewhere to join in, but an isolated newcomer may find himself being wooed by one or two cliques in order to get him on their side.

In a healthy staffroom, alliances and groupings will form and reform; you may agree with a colleague on one point but disagree on another. A most unpleasant atmosphere develops in a staffroom divided into cliques. I am sure that other professions may suffer at times from cliquiness, and resentment of the supposed power of the in-group. It may be that where teachers have allowed themselves to become isolated in school, with division from their pupils by a Them-Us mentality, they may become prone to this hard group formation as a desperate means of finding support. It is not, let me be quite adamant, an inevitable part of the teacher's lot.

In spite of this danger, and in spite of the stereotype that others may construct for 'the typical teacher', the profession seems to me to remain obdurately full of individuals. Individuals between whom there may be some similarities, but the variety in a staff-room will be nearly as marked as that shown among any bus-full of people going about their daily business. As in other working groups, of course, we often cast individuals in roles that they then feel they must play out, as, the barrack-room lawyer, the starry-eyed idealist, the misogynist, the reactionary. Some conform, if only to oblige, like the Scottish cynic I worked with who always took students and probationers aside for his one piece of advice —'Never smile before Easter.' Others struggle, like Marcel Marceau's mask-maker, to break free. A friend recently said 'I'm tired now of coming into the staffroom and have them say "We're feeling low, Bill, come and cheer us up".' He was a hilarious raconteur, but realised he was being restricted by the others to his role of joker, and he wanted to break out of it. We all need to play several parts and he was not content to be stuck with just one.

The way in which a newcomer to a school sees any other teacher there will also depend on function within the framework of responsibilities. Schools vary in the degree to which their hier-archies are marked or reinforced, but whether there is an open, egalitarian style of address or a pecking order revealed by who speaks to whom, nearly every school maintains a structure of function that can be outlined fairly simply.

Almost invariably that structure will be determined by the head teacher and it will reflect his or her style of operating. The head teacher is a phenomenon deserving a separate section and will appear more fully in Chapter 4. But whether the head's mode of operation is bureaucratic or charismatic, it will only be effective through the structures of the staff.

By tradition in British schools, teachers take on a dual respon-sibility, for learning and for social care. This is in contrast to other national traditions. In France, for instance, the teacher is the 'professeur' who delivers his lessons and expects his tasks to be carried out, but is not in the least 'in loco parentis' as we are. Not for him the worries of recommending that Jack has free clothing or Jill has advice about period pains. If his pupils smoke Disque Bleu or spray slogans on the bus shelter that is their parents' concern and none of his. With us it is ordered differently. We pride ourselves on trying to treat each pupil as a known and cared for individual. At its best this care is real, though too often it degenerates into moralising and chivvying. So every teacher will be concerned both with his pupils' learning within the curriculum, and with their social well-being. Institutionally, we tend to differentiate these two major responsibilities.

The head is held responsible for the lot, but he will usually delegate areas of this responsibility and the areas tend to be seen as either those of curriculum, the subject disciplines, or those of pastoral care. Every head, except in the minutest of rural schools, has a deputy, and in most schools will have two. In a mixed school it is required that where there are two deputies they should be one of either sex. How they are expected to function will turn to a large extent on personality, but it is wise for a head to be sure that one of them, at least, can deputise in the true sense of standing in during absence for whatever tasks might have fallen to the head if present, whether meeting a worried parent or answering a query from the local press.

The provision for two deputies only came into effect in 1971. It provides for a better balance. All too often the single deputy had the invidious tasks of doing the head's chores and dirty work, while acting as go-between with the staff. Timetables, duty lists, coverage of absences, checking registers, medical inspections, niggles with cleaning staff and the school meals supervisor were all within the compass of the deputy's office, coupled with the daily crop of disciplinary problems referred by others on the staff. I would sometimes encounter Marjorie Dickson, deputy head at Crown Woods, gasping for breath at the top of a staircase to tell me in amused exasperation 'I once thought a degree in Classics would be relevant to me as a teacher, but I have long since abandoned the idea.' And off she would charge to track down some girl said to be smoking in the toilets. Miss Dickson was the most tenacious woman I ever knew, but one who could tell a story against herself. She told us once how she was so determined to catch a girl who wouldn't come out of a lavatory when she called her that she sent for the caretaker to bring a pair of steps so that she could confront her over the door, only to discover that she was involved in the new craze for locking a cubicle door and then crawling out under the bottom. The loo was vacant.

A pair of deputies allows the head to divide the delegation, and the most usual pattern is for one to oversee curriculum and related aspects, while the other co-ordinates the pastoral or welfare duties. Where the division is rigid it can be wasteful: no good teacher having reached the level of deputy is going to be satisfied with leaving one half of his or her experience untapped. That Classics degree should have some relevance, just as knowledge of how the twelve-year-old ticks, or fails to tick, must not go unused. Nevertheless, in management terms, this way of dividing the labour can work well enough. Where one deputy is responsible for the co-ordination of subject disciplines he is now often classified as Director of Studies, a term brought into secondary schooling by Malcolm Ross when at Crown Woods he appointed someone to replace a senior master in 1959 and needed a man of a new organising capacity, able to co-ordinate and develop the department of study. (It was an imaginative decision and it brought him Peter Cornall, who has since shown himself a brilliant innovator both as education officer and headmaster.)

A deputy as Director of Studies will be the head's link with the departments. Senior posts in a school will be filled by heads of the departments of English, Maths, Sciences, Languages, Art, Crafts, Music, Physical Education, History, Geography and Religious Education. The relative degrees of importance attached to these by the head will be reflected in the size of additional allowances on salary paid to each. The maintaining authority pays teachers by agreement with the Burnham Committee, but their

34

distribution of additional allowances, agreed in number and amount according to size of school also with Burnham, is carried out virtually on the recommendation of the head teacher. Schools are altering the shape of curriculum so that we sometimes find that traditional subjects become swallowed up, merge or at any rate lose their identity. Thus English and Maths remain as the central pillars of curriculum, with heads of these departments receiving the largest additional allowances, while we may find that the sciences have been differentiated, each with its own head, paid a somewhat lower allowance; or we may find that History, Geography and Religious Education have been integrated with a senior teacher designated Head of Humanities, or of Combined Studies, or Social Studies. There may remain recognised teachers in charge of the separate subjects, such as Needlework, Commerce, Technical Drawing and so on, but their position in the hierarchy, and the importance that is seen to attach to their subject will be reflected in their allowances. There are exceptions, as a head will tend to offer attractive allowances where there is a shortage of specialists and he is recruiting from the open market. We find that a teacher of Chemistry can usually command a higher price than a teacher of Woodwork, not only because the chemist is likely to be a graduate and paid for it, but because an additional allowance may be going for the post.

The Director of Studies therefore has a huge task co-ordinating this number of major and minor subjects in a secondary school. Communications alone present a problem, and some heads have rationalised the situation by limiting the number of senior departmental heads to sit on the central decision-making cabinet. When head of Banbury School, Harry Judge quirkily called these teachers 'the barons'. At West Bridgford, Peter Cornall established a central directorate of four directors to cover between them the whole academic work. A Director of Creative Arts was responsible for Art, Craft, Home Economics, Music, Technical Studies. A Director of Language Studies was responsible for English, Classics and Modern Languages. There was a Director of Mathematical and Scientific Studies, and the Director of World Studies co-ordinated Geography, History, Religious Education and Economics.

The head of department, and to an even greater degree a director on the West Bridgford pattern, will carry responsibility for keeping the channel of communication open between the head's cabinet and the teachers in his subject or cluster of subjects. The communication should be two-way, which will only be achieved if he arranges regularly to hold open discussion with his sector of the staff. In a large school, such a departmental meeting might call twenty teachers together, though a department might consist of only two or three. For efficient management it seems to be good sense to link under some kind of 'overlord' the small subjects such as Technical Drawing or Greek that might have only one specialist teacher. On the other hand, it makes it even more likely that that teacher of TD or Greek is going to remain feeling a small cog in the machine of efficient management.

However, as well as being a subject specialist, or even having simply a main subject commitment amongst others, the assistant teacher will have pastoral responsibility. The commonest scheme of pastoral care is based on the tutor or form teacher unit. This provides for the pupils to be divided into groups of about thirty with one teacher attached to them for their general arrangement and welfare. This form teacher will see the class each morning to check attendance and appearance, may collect dinner money and other dues, receive letters from home explaining absence or requesting light duties. Here we are at the grass roots of teacher-pupil relationships and can observe the conditions of contact, understanding and trust that make learning possible, or if those conditions are bad, make learning unlikely and hostility probable.

In a primary school this link between tutorship and teaching is tight and strong because the tutor is also the form's teacher for most of its working time. The duality of the British teacher's role is held together. But if in primary school these two roles, pastor and teacher, coincide, in secondary school they often scarcely intersect. If the form teacher sees his form as a specialist teacher, then he may teach them for five or six of the forty periods in a week if his is a major subject like Maths, or only one or two periods if his specialism is Geography or Religious Education. But it is possible that he never teaches them at all, either because the timetable has placed him in some quite different teaching area, or because his tutorial group re-forms for different subjects so that only two or three of them may remain together for the subject that their tutor teaches them. This dilemma is common in the large school, but not inevitable, as I shall show later. Where it does exist though, it reduces the effectiveness of the pastoral role required of the teacher, because in the end the most effective way of getting to know your charges is to teach them.

No head with a school of over two hundred pupils can honestly claim to know all his pupils. (He may know them all by name, even a thousand of them, but that is only an effort of reassurance or a piece of showmanship, since he cannot possibly know them.) He therefore relies on the framework of tutors to see that each pupil is known individually. The tutor must be able to learn the personal oddities and hang-ups of each of his thirty charges, to know something of their home background and their standards of achievement across the subjects of the curriculum. When the head wants to know how Janet Smith is getting on, it is to the tutor that he must refer for the summary report that collates all the assessments of her various subject teachers. But a secondary school may have any number of classes, from twenty to eighty, each with its tutor. The head cannot conveniently correlate the knowledge of all these tutors, but will rely on a second structure, separate from that of academic departments, to organise the pastoral care of the school.

The most influential model of pastoral care in British schools has been provided by the boarding house of the traditional public school. Here were houses, literally, that supplied the home needs of a group of boys, living together as a large family with the housemaster and his wife acting as surrogate parents. The cohesion among members of a house was powerful, producing a loyalty which could even transcend the personality of the housemaster himself, reifying 'the house' as an institution, and rendering competition between the houses of one school intense.

The effectiveness of the house system at public boarding schools led to the adoption in day schools of an imitative pattern, dividing pupils into a number of units which were then called 'houses', each under the care of a housemaster or housemistress. These were useful as more manageable groupings for individual care: with no more than two hundred in a 'house', the house teacher could know the pupils in a way that the head teacher could not hope to. It was a forlorn hope ever to expect that houses in a day school would foster the loyalty and competitiveness of their boarding school forebears, and yet endless amounts of time, energy and empty oratory have gone into whipping up damp enthusiasm over house matches and house points. Particularly in large schools, the intention was to induce for each pupil a sense of loyalty and identity to a group that was within imaginative grasp. All too often the pupil has seen the apparatus of house colours, 'traditions' and appeals to a sense of duty, as a charade thinly masking an administrative convenience.

An administrative convenience it certainly is, as it enables the form tutors to group under a Head of House who then can pass pastoral concerns to the deputy and the head, while reciprocally passing down the policy over discipline, reports and so on. The heads of houses are of course subject teachers in their own right but, particularly in a large school, are not likely to carry also the load of a head of department. In the development period of the comprehensive schools, the head of house posts offered a convenient position of status for older and experienced men and women who lacked the academic qualifications expected of heads of departments. They thus tended to form the most conservative element in the staffroom, vulnerable and therefore defensive, less accustomed to academic dispute and therefore authoritarian. A head would often call them the backbone of his staff. Some others

have called them the brick wall against which they were banging
their heads.

An alternative to the house system as a means of breaking the
school down into more manageable units, is a system of year-
teachers. In our jargon, this is a horizontal organisation as opposed
to the vertical, house system. The year-teacher will be responsible
for co-ordinating what is known by tutors across a whole age
group. A housemaster in the vertical organisation can compare
one age with another but cannot know more children in any one
year than he has in his house. The year-master can decide on the
form membership and recommend changes so that a pupil may
transfer to a different form. In the vertical system, house heads
could only effect such a change in class membership in consultation
with all the other house heads. There are other advantages, such
as the teacher responsible for the first year being able to consult
the contributory primary schools instead of all the house heads
being involved, and the fifth-year teacher being able to organise
examinations or youth employment. The horizontal system puts
about the same number of pupils under the guidance of the teacher
responsible as does a house in the vertical organisation. The main
distinction is that the horizontal system emphasises practical and
individual pastoral care, tied closely to the balancing of the individual's curriculum, while the vertical house system emphasises
control and competitiveness.

And so even if most of the work carried out by an assistant
teacher takes place in the isolation of the classroom, he is operating
within a system of teams. He may resist and resent this, having a
head of house or year-teacher telling him to send him a pink form
naming any pupil who has been away unaccountably for two
days, and a head of department telling him which textbook to
use in conjunction with which syllabus with which form. Or he
may welcome the support, given by the team within which he is
working, either because he has problems that may be helped by
sharing, or simply because he recognises that two heads are
better than one when it comes to ideas. How he takes it will

depend partly on personal temperament, and partly on the way in which the middle-management staff handle their teams.

By the time a teacher has trained and taken up an appointment in school, he or she may reasonably expect to be regarded by colleagues as of sufficient maturity and intelligence to deserve consultation and a share of responsibility. All too often the regard paid in this respect is insufficient, the new teacher being treated more like an apprentice, or a raw recruit who still has to get his knees brown. How and why this treatment of junior staff must change, I raise in a later chapter. But where the junior members are enabled to feel any real stake and voice in the nature of the school situation which they find themselves in, it is through the teams and the extent to which they participate in them.

In a school of only twenty or thirty staff, it is still just possible for the head to conduct a staff meeting in which discussion can take place. Above that number and often enough even within it, staff meetings tend to be unwieldy affairs in which it is only possible to issue orders or make statements. Such a way of conducting affairs is not enough to bring commitment to the school and its policies, except amongst the submissive and lazy minded. For real commitment, the individual needs to feel party, in some measure at least, to the decisions that affect the conditions of work.

Unfortunately, the habit of school teachers in their main function of teaching in class has been to dictate the conditions of work to their pupils, paying scant regard, if any at all, to what they may think about the whole business, and when given responsibility for the work of a number of his colleagues a teacher will tend to treat them in the same authoritarian manner as he previously treated his pupils. If, however, the man or woman appointed to seniority can be made aware of this, or if, better still, they actually have taught in class in such a way that pupils did contribute to the way in which lessons occurred, the departmental and house teams can begin to operate co-operatively.

The authoritarian middle-management teacher will rely on bureaucratic control, by employing such techniques as issuing directives by paper message, or by hurried encounter in corridor, or on the way into assembly, when there is no chance of come-back. I have known a house head whose technique for commiting staff to her policy was to make an announcement to pupils in the presence of house tutors and then add the rider, 'And I'm sure all the house staff here agree, isn't that so?' It was then all but impossible to express disagreement.

The consultative team leader, or director, will tend to operate by more open group discussion. He may still need to issue direc-tives on details—'Return all textbooks to stock room by break on the last morning.' But the policy and philosophy of the team will be hammered out in open discussion. This means that the team leader will need to hold meetings of the teachers in his department, or house, or year. He will need to keep his ears open for the rumbles that denote uncertainties, lack of direction, so that he may draw up an appropriate agenda and prepare for discussion so that he is not caught unprepared. He should be ready to do a lot of listening and confine his advice until it is really needed. All this would be true of a head teacher, and indeed, the members of middle management will, to a more restricted degree only need to exhibit many of the qualities of a head.

These then are the main permanent frameworks of a school within which an assistant teacher operates. These are inescapable. Over and above these exist numerous other temporary and voluntary coalitions in which he may relate to colleagues. He joins a group that is organising a journey of pupils to the Alps; he is coerced into being publicity manager for the school play; he becomes secretary of the staff theatre-visits club; stars in the school *v* staff hockey match; offers to do the whip-round for young Maggie Barnet who is leaving to have a baby; is selected to organise a tour around school of a party of college students.

How the teacher relates to his colleagues collectively, as an assembled staff, may be seen more clearly when I look in Chapter 4 at styles of school. Some schools very rarely have meetings for the whole staff, at many others they are seen as a necessary evil, while for some they offer real hope of affecting policy and practice. Certainly, individuals on a staff may play specific roles at staff meetings that are not generally apparent at other times, indeed such roles may be assumed only for public display. One may be spokesman, possibly self-appointed, for the iron-guard disciplinarians; another may be the voice of sweetness and light; one may stand as the hammer of the educational theorists; there are those who will say what they think the head wants to hear, and those who will say what they think the head's radical opponents want to hear. There are also, of course, those who will just give an honest opinion when they think it may be of some use. But teachers, like most others, and especially the articulate, take on different colours and dimensions when launching into public statement. Anyone with any sense, let alone a streak of cynicism, will watch to see how far a colleague's protestations in staff meetings match his actions in practice when the preaching is over.

One of the standard risks for a teacher lies in his isolation at work from the rest of the adult world. Yet the isolation is not complete, nor even dependent on the irregular contact with parents. Very much part of any school life are the caretaker, his cleaners, the clerical staff, the dinner ladies and, increasingly now, non-teaching ancillaries.

The head sometimes manages to have a private secretary, but more often there is a secretary who is general to the school. She is usually the first contact anyone makes with school, whether they are phoning in or calling personally, so that the school stands to gain or lose an enormous amount in reputation for its attitude from its secretary. If she is curt or officious, the caller may become hostile, feel offended, or scared off. But if she is friendly in tone, sympathetic to the doubts and worries of callers, can put them at ease if they are waiting, the response is quite other. As a head I have been in a better position to watch the effects, over a period of time, of having a welcoming and understanding secretary. These human qualities are responded to by the tradesmen, visiting officers from County Hall, policemen, and all the others who call, but above all by parents. For many parents, school contact arouses the most deep-seated anxieties, both because of long-held resentments from their own school days when meeting the head was inevitably associated with trouble, and because their approach as parents to the school is likely to be over worries for their children, whom they entrust to these teachers, whom they may hardly know. May we be forgiven at schools, as at hospitals, for the number of humble, inarticulate parents who have been sent home silent and sick with worry about their child by a super-efficient receptionist, when a warm word from someone who identified with them could have left them feeling all was well, that 'they' were human after all. Give me any day at school a secretary who sees herself essentially as one with the parents, and best of all, actually is one of the parents. She is the best possible public relations officer a school could have. Thank you Mrs Wynn, Joan Hillier, Dorothy Clark.

A large school will normally have a bursar, or administrator, who relieves the head of most of the paper work involved in returns, school meals, building maintenance, finance and orders. In a small school, all this may fall to the head, though if he allows himself to become enmeshed in it rather than delegating it, he is either incompetent or secretly enjoying it. The bursar is often someone on detachment from County Hall, with knowledge of all the regulations and dodges, as well as the contacts with the other officers there whose goodwill is needed to keep things moving. No teacher can afford to be impatient of the bursar's pride in his contacts and subterfuges, his ability to 'get on the blower to old Phelps up there in school supplies. Know him well enough to get him to hurry things up a bit.' You only have to try once to get something out of the administration without knowledge of the proper human channels to appreciate having someone to hand who has that access. And there is equally no denying the value to anyone who comes out from County Hall as a school admin. officer, who runs into the teachers direct and who sees the 'educational units' turned into boys and girls with individual faces. I have known them even end up joining the staff taking pupils off on school journeys.

Even the smallest school has its caretaker to reckon with: in fact, the smaller the school, the more powerful the caretaker is likely to become. He very often lives on the site. He controls the hours of opening. He arranges the furniture and maintains the heating system. No head teacher should disregard the feelings of the caretaker or fail to safeguard his prerogatives. A hostile caretaker can force a school to work to rule and chill its spirit to the marrow, and yet it is amazing to find how regularly he is someone with a pride and dedication that could shame many a teacher. I have known caretakers who will make the scenery and props for a play, who will keep the staffroom as a home instead of a jumble room for teachers, or who would maintain portable heaters in every room sooner than see the school close because his boilers had broken down. Some of the pioneer audio-visual technical assistants in schools were their caretakers with a flair for gadgetry. He is often feared and respected by children in a way that makes an unprepossessing teacher envious, and indeed he may complain sotto voce about the lack of control shown by some of these young teachers. But then many a caretaker was a retired NCO and the tradition lingers on.

I knew of one caretaker, an ex-sergeant major who ran a cadet unit for local boys, until one evening, before a visiting inspecting officer, he flung himself into the prone position to demonstrate how to fire a Bren gun and put a short burst clean through the back wall of the classroom. The bullets passed through the cupboard under the blackboard in the classroom next door. The classroom was empty fortunately, but the cupboard was where the class teacher kept his violin and the caretaker's short burst travelled through that too.

In London, the caretaker is dubbed 'schoolkeeper' and wears a uniform only less impressive than that of a city messenger. In a large school, the head schoolkeeper may command a regiment of assistants. He is likely to come from a long line of schoolkeepers, as did Frank Dossett, the most impressive one I knew. His father had been a schoolkeeper for LCC before him, and his son was another after him. When I arrived at Crown Woods to be interviewed by the governors for the headship of their English Department in 1958, Frank Dossett met me, chatted me up, escorted me to the library where the interview was to be, and told me 'You'll get this.' I asked him how he could know. 'I've seen 'em come and seen 'em go,' he said. Perhaps he said this to each candidate, but I think not. When he retired he was awarded the CBE.

Lab assistants, typists, kitchen staff, librarians all go to leaven that body of teachers, which might otherwise be so much more like a lump of dough. They bring the realities in to school through its back doors and are often ignored by the very teachers who proclaim that we should open the school to the world outside. Too often they are divided from the teachers by sheer snobbery disguised as professional standing. Where a school has the support of its non-teaching staff, the teachers could do well to acknowledge the strength this gives to them. They could then afford to drop the condescending patronage of collecting for a Christmas box for the kitchen and cleaning staff, many of whom they would discover to be parents if they bothered to find out, and instead open their staff common room at all times to these others. The idea would horrify some of my old Jerseymen colleagues, and their like up and down the country, but only strength would result eventually from regarding all the people in schools as having a community of interest and recognising it with a sharing of amenities.

# CHAPTER THREE

# In the Classroom

A Boy's Head

In it there is a space-ship
and a project
for doing away with piano lessons.

And there is
Noah's ark,
which shall be first.

And there is
an entirely new bird,
an entirely new hare,
an entirely new bumble bee.

There is a river
that flows upwards

There is a multiplication table.

There is anti-matter.
And it just cannot be trimmed.

I believe
that only what cannot be trimmed
is a head.

There is much promise
in the circumstance
that so many people have heads.

MIROSLAV HOLUB

But the teacher will not have any immediate insight into what is going on inside the boy's head. What he experiences on first walking into a strange class will be very different. He may, if the general control system of the school is effective, be met by thirty stony stares and be given a silent scrutiny. This is very unnerving unless the teacher has acquired the techniques of dealing with it immediately by plunging the class straight into some exercise that will occupy them without puzzling them. The temptation is to embark on some chatty introduction 'to get to know them'. This is fatal as it only lets them get to know you, while ruining any chance of getting them down to work. I always warned a student on practice that it would take a week or two to know much about a class, but that they would have sized you up in five minutes flat.

They may wait for you to give yourself away, whether by a remark like, 'I hope we are all going to be good friends in my lessons', which tells them that they have got a right soft one here, or by something like 'Books out. Date in the top right corner. Those without pen or pencil place their hands on top of their heads', in which case the battle is on. They may, on the other hand, take the initiative and try you out, by some such device as insisting, when you ask for their names, that they are all called Jones, or Bobby Charlton.

If you do not start with the supportive framework of a well ordered school, you may not receive such a controlled test period. The initiation can be an ordeal by fire. I have stepped into an inner London comprehensive school classroom to start work with a class on my first morning with them only to find that my first task was to round up the thirteen-year-olds meant to be there, and then drive them into the room. Half of them sat at desks in apathetic silence while the other half ran around the room shouting encouragements to the two huge girls belabouring each other with their truncheon-like umbrellas. The decision to remove the two offensive weapons had to be taken in the knowledge that they might be succeeded by knives. Persistence and a refusal to be rattled gradually won enough order for work to commence, but that was a Monday morning. On a Friday afternoon, intervention might have been more cautious.

However, once the introductions are over, the teacher will be trying to divine those movements within the boy's head. He will try to follow this transmutation of facts into fantasies, and to mesh whatever he has to offer to its capricious wheelings. The teacher should be less concerned with what he is teaching than with what his pupil is learning. Too often the teacher has been thought of as the one who knows, pouring his knowledge into the head of the receptive pupil, who in turn ends up, under ideal conditions, knowing all that his teacher knew, a replica mind like a blank disc that has been pressed by the master record (significant that 'master') and can give perfect reproduction. All the pupil is supposed to do is give the master his attention, and obey his direction, failure being largely attributable to inattention, wilfulness, stupidity or a combination of all three.

This was not what Socrates thought was happening in the teaching process. By his teaching he sought to draw out from his disciple what was already in him in potential, activating his power of reason so that the latent became apparent and the learner 'saw'. This capacity to make the learner 'see' has always been recognised as the teacher's crucial skill. Plato in *The Republic* told the parable of the prisoners in the cave who only saw reality represented by the shadows of objects cast by firelight on the walls of their prison. They never saw these objects, or the living things they were modelled on, until someone came to turn their heads in the right direction and eventually to lead them out of the cave altogether into the light where they could see things as they really were.

Leading the seeker to see for himself is the teacher's task, and his principal reward. The greatest teaching heresy has been to believe that the teacher mastered his pupil and stamped his knowledge on to his impressionable mind as if it were a piece of blank wax.

In Europe, Holland and Switzerland had each introduced compulsory popular education before Waterloo in 1815, with Prussia following almost at the same time. Their main influence in approach came from Pestalozzi in Switzerland, for whom education was essentially child-centred, the teacher seen as the gardener who nurtured the growing plant. In England, where popular compulsory education was to wait for another half a century, a need was nevertheless seen for wider, more efficient schooling and the need produced the man, Andrew Bell.

Bell was possibly the greatest disaster in the history of education. He was conceited, overbearing, uncharitable, but he got things done—a fatal combination. With his partner Lancaster he developed the notorious Bell and Lancaster monitorial system. It bore all the hallmarks of efficiency and inhumanity that we associate with the growing industrialism of that time and was indeed a limb of that same monster. Essentially, Bell's system arranged for the master's instruction of a first wave of élite pupils to be passed on by them as monitors to a second wave who in turn instructed a third wave. Presumably at some stage the nuggets of information became so distorted as to be no longer worth passing on, but it was thought quite possible for one master in this manner to instruct one thousand pupils dragooned into one hall. Of course they had to be disciplined into order, which was done by ushers moving about with long switches to swish the inattentive and idle into obedience. It was a travesty of education, reducing understanding to rote learning, processing children like so much raw material, eliminating the possibility of a trusting relationship between teacher and student. But it worked: it could mass-produce low-level clerks and semi-skilled operatives. And Bell was a salesman. He toured Europe, not like his contemporary Robert Owen, to learn, but to advise. He was not impressed by Pestalozzi, whom he found 'against emulation'. But never mind Switzerland; it was the nations that knew the Duke of Wellington, France and Spain, that first bought Bell's methods, and from there his system of 'mutual instruction' spread rapidly to Italy, Greece and Scandinavia.

We have not yet undone the damage done by Bell to the concept of popular education in this country. Gradually, the humane teaching of men like Pestalozzi and Froebel have had their effect, but delayed by a hundred years and suspect for being foreign. Popular education became inseparably linked after Bell to efficient production of dehumanised artisans. In 1854 Dickens attacked the Bell and Lancaster approach brilliantly in *Hard Times*, exposing the direct relationship of such schooling to the crushing inhumanity of industry. His portraits of Mr Gradgrind and Mr M'Choakumchild still stand as the most withering criticism of teaching as fact grinding ever written.

Even the introduction of compulsory elementary education by W. E. Forster in 1870 was clearly intended to promote the position of Britain as an industrial power as much as to benefit the children who were being viciously exploited by employers in industry. 'What is our purpose in this Bill?' asked Forster. 'Briefly this, to bring elementary education within the reach of every English home, aye, and within the reach of those children who have no homes . . .' Which is fine, but he went on, 'Upon this speedy provision of elementary education depends our industrial prosperity.' And from the curriculum and method adopted, it is clear that Forster's conclusion was the operative part, with the main aim that of producing literate and more skilled industrial workers.

All this was a very far cry from Pestalozzi and Froebel, from any conception of education as the means of the individual child's coming to know itself and its relationship to the world. In 1826, Froebel wrote 'The child should learn early how to find in himself the centre and fulcrum of all his powers and members.' Far from the teacher directing the pupil's actions, he should be encouraging him to discover truths for himself. The teacher may arrange conditions so as to maximise the possibility of such discovery, but the experience had to be the child's own. 'The school, as such, implies the presence of an intelligent consciousness which, as it were, hovers over and between the outer world and the scholar, which unites in itself the essence of both, mediating between the two.' (Friedrich Froebel, *The Education of Man*, 1826.)

But for us English, though the notion of that mediating, hovering sort of teacher might apply to a university tutor, it was so much Romantic moonshine when we took a cool look at the general herd compelled into school attendance. They were a rough bunch, in no way overjoyed at the benefits being conferred upon them. They needed to learn their letters, do their sums, show respect to their masters and be grateful for their daily bread. And under Bell's baleful influence the teachers knew that they were well able to administer an elementary instruction of that kind. It was from the start an instrumental form of education, that is, schooling that was considered little for its intrinsic value in fostering the growth of a pupil, but essentially for the qualification it gave at the end. It was all very well for the gentry to regard a good book as 'the life blood of a master spirit', but the labourer's son needed to ask more pertinently whether it was going to enable him to get a better job.

And so it is that to this very day, the teacher in his classroom is held in tension between the popular expectation that he will drill his pupils so that he gets them through their exams, and his professional or vocational commitment to aiding each and every pupil towards self-knowledge, self-fulfilment. We have already looked at one kind of duality in the teacher's role, that of subject teacher combined with pastoral care. Now let us re-examine it as a strain between the demands for instrumental utilitarian teaching and the professional obligation to foster individual growth.

The teacher will normally base the organisation of class time on the requirements of a subject, or a series of subjects. Even in primary schools, where a higher degree of integration of subjects, activities and periods of the day is likely to be found than in secondary schools, what the pupils are engaged upon will depend in nature upon the subject. A subject, Maths, History, say, or Art, is a way of ordering experience, a way of understanding, that is distinguished from other ways. A subject is a way of looking at things and of doing: it carries its own discipline, in fact is sometimes called 'a discipline', rather than a subject. It seems to be axiomatic that in constructing the curriculum, ie the totality of planned situations in which learning may occur, teachers need to balance opportunities for as many different ways as possible of experiencing and interpreting. Hence the broad, subject-based curriculum.

However, the subject can easily assert its own tyranny by accumulating subject matter. The teacher is then forced to set aside ways of interpreting experience in favour of a body of accepted knowledge. This secondhand knowledge and replication of other people's experience comes in the form of a syllabus. A subject is already dead when the teacher is working through a syllabus. And yet for many schoolchildren, their education is reduced to the absorption of dead knowledge through a set of dead subjects. Some teachers base their professional pride on how thoroughly they can drive their students through a syllabus, measuring their success finally by examination results; some pride themselves on the speed with which they can get the syllabus out of the way, so that they may proceed to some more enjoyable and experimental work; others would claim that the true value of their teaching lay in what was learnt by their students over and above the syllabus as they went along, the way of thinking, peculiar to the subject, that was rubbing off on to them throughout the process.

All that a subject syllabus or test of progress needs to ask of a student, or expect a teacher to have done for him, is to show evidence of having learnt to interpret experience in the mode of that subject. This puts the onus on the teacher to understand his subject in the first place, as a particular way of seeing, and to arrange for his students to have experiences which he can teach them how to interpret. The skill of the teacher lies in this How. If he does not feel this How in his bones, then he is reduced to teaching What. He takes to presenting what other people experienced and how they interpreted it. If he is enterprising he will compile his own collection of examples and he may develop an entertainer's skill at presenting these in a manner said to be interesting. But this is the empty technique of the instructor and still not teaching. More usually though, the compilation will have been done by yet another person and the teacher is then reduced to working through a given syllabus. In History, for instance, this means that instead of the teacher explaining the nature of historical evidence, dating artifacts, examining documents and drawing conclusions so that his students can actually do this, he has to present other people's conclusions and oblige his pupils to memorise definitions of abstractions like Feudalism, or learn by heart the causes and effects of the Civil War, according to the period laid down by the syllabus. Learning becomes displaced by disjointed information, by Mr Gradgrind's facts. It is an indictment of our educational system that success is so often measured by sheer power of recall of information which on its own is quite useless. Television abounds with asinine programmes such as 'Brain of Britain' where aimless regurgitation of dates, dimensions, names, are hailed as the marks of genius. It is significant, as was recently pointed out to me, how obsessed grammar-school pupils can become with the notion of someone's possessing photographic memory. If only one had this gift of the gods, it is supposed, all exams would be passable and all the benefits of education assured. I really don't believe that in this age of instant photocopiers and microfilm or transistorised data retrieval, anyone outside the O and A rat-race worries their head about photographic memory. 'Where is the wisdom we have lost in knowledge? Where is the knowledge we have lost in information?'

We tend to blame the requirements of examining boards and in particular the universities mediated by the Advanced and Ordinary levels ('A' and 'O' levels) of the General Certificate of Education (GCE). It is true that the syllabuses of these exams, in conjunction with the ambitions of students and more especially their parents, squeeze out most opportunities for real learning, except for the fastest workers. But we must also accept the condemnation of those many teachers for whom examinations are a prop, which once removed would cause impossible demands upon their ingenuity and imagination to come tumbling down on their heads.

However, while syllabuses remain, the teacher has to devote more time to organising coverage and to testing for progress than to real teaching. Where he can escape the tyranny, he can allow the work of a class, or groups within the class to develop without having to watch the clock so closely. True explorations of experience need time. This does not relieve the teacher of the need to organise. Just as much as when forced to work to a controlled syllabus, the teacher in the open situation must be organised. In fact he must be all the more organised since he faces the spontaneous and unexpected development. And in addition to that, whereas syllabus-tracking tends to require students to produce similar outcomes and cover identical ground at identical speeds, open work usually results in individuals and groups following different routes at different rates, all of which the teacher has to monitor and service.

In syllabus-based teaching, the conscientious teacher concentrates on making clear to each pupil what he is expected to know. The pupil does not initiate the study, the syllabus does. If the teacher displays an interest in the subject and takes care to see that each pupil understands each stage before being introduced to the next, then he may win pupils' respect and motivate them to assimilate what they need to know. But for most pupils, the motivation will spring from that need for the qualifying exam result, not from any interest aroused by the study itself. Remove the examination, or desire for success in it, and what motivation can remain for them? Even with the exam, if it is not looming large and the student is able to postpone its worry, the teacher may find him undermotivated. He is then expected to drive the pupil: parents frequently demand that their children be driven, saying 'He won't work unless he's made to. He needs pushing.' It all adds up to a general belief that learning is a bore, that children are inherently lazy, and that teachers must inescapably be harsh task-masters, or at least effective task-masters.

All this has been of our own making, and of course will continue for as long as adults build up by a million implications, the myth that learning is a bore and teacher is an ogre, or at best a strict philanthropist. It need not be. And where the good teacher is allowed to practise his art undisturbed by the hectoring of over-ambitious parents, results-conscious headmasters or faceless examiners, the real learning happens.

It may happen in the classroom, or it may take class and teacher outside into the highways and byways. It will be where the teacher has enabled boys and girls to watch, listen, feel, record, reflect and celebrate the world around them. It can only happen when the pupils trust their teacher, trust him to know each as an individual, trust him to know what he is doing and have the competence to carry the work through, trust him to tolerate mistakes patiently, trust him to recognise achievement relative to the individual (as distinct from some arbitrary level that divides them inexplicably into passes and failures, labelling some as 'having it up there', and others as 'dimmies').

Given this trust, then children are not afraid of exposing their ignorance by asking why and how things happen or are like they are. The human mind is intrinsically motivated to inquire and learn: only adults can suppress this desire for understanding.

The good teacher then will constantly be making opportunities for firsthand experience. He and his pupils will bring things into school, the sorts of things that tend to upset tidy housewives and are therefore probably banned at home: furry things like rats, dirty things like motor-bike engines, slimy things like frog spawn, smelly things like wild garlic. And they will make untidy messes by seeing what happens when you turn a rat loose, or lubricate a crankshaft, or hatch out tadpoles, or boil wild plants to make dye. But out of the mess and activity will come the questions that induce study: rats on the loose may lead to Biology and Psychology, crankshafts to Metallurgy, frog spawn to Genetics, dyes to Chemistry or Botany. And on the way the teacher will encourage recording of results in writing, in statistics, in photography, in painting, in talk.

At primary school, one teacher may be able to cope with all this diversity, so that the classroom is a workshop where the walls are a gallery and models fly from the ceiling. In secondary school, the teacher is more likely to develop his own subject specialism in depth and leave his colleagues to the others. Ideally, the specialists will relate what they do and enable a student to pursue his interests between them. It can be done, but it is unfortunately rare. More usually the student follows the separate subjects and is lucky to stitch together even a few of the fragments.

The teacher does not need to rely on what can be experienced only in school. He will make frequent excursions. These are the occasions when you see your pupils in quite new lights. You may take them to collect frog spawn so that questions may arise from discovering it in its natural place, and that quiet boy who seemed interested in so little may turn out to be the local expert in locating spawning pools. You may take them to a workshop to see car engines being stripped down because one of your girls has a father who is the foreman mechanic there. And nothing teaches one faster than being thrust into the position of the expert who has to explain what one thought was obvious to those who are ignorant. There was the fourteen-year-old boy who found all writing tough going but held me and class spellbound for forty minutes describing the whole process of the slaughterhouse where he worked at weekends and holidays. The girls in the class dissuaded us from taking up his invitation to arrange a visit with his boss.

Whether going out or staying in, the teacher must be able to employ skills of management. In the days when chalk and talk dominated the classroom, there was little to manage except for the chalk supply and cleaning the duster (operations which many of us will remember our teacher elaborating to all but ritual level). Chalk and talk have far from disappeared, but for the most part developments require that a teacher organise his work in much more complex ways. He needs to be able to organise space, time, materials and people. So much more is available to him than in former times that he needs to know how to bring it all into operation if it is not to be wasted or if it is not to bring confusion into his work.

Space needs organising once you realise that there is no obligation to keep pupils rooted each to a given place in the formal rows of desks. (Not forgetting that many teachers do feel obliged by their headmasters to keep their rooms like that.) Of course, if the teacher remains on a dais between his desk and blackboard, teaching by addressing the whole class and demanding their simultaneous attention, then a formal arrangement in rows may suit him (though if only they would build them for us, a quarter-circle in stepped tiers would be far more appropriate to a lecturing approach). But nowadays the lecture is likely to make a very limited appearance in classwork, and the teacher may rearrange his seating. It is more likely in a primary school, and increasingly likely in secondary school, that work will be proceeding with pupils collaborating in small groups or singly. An appropriate seating arrangement for this will be with desks turned inwards in clusters, with some for individuals turned outwards to wall or window.

Not only the desks and tables but also equipment and expendable materials need to be organised spatially so that they are safe but accessible. The teacher needs to be able to organise his room like a workshop, and anyone thinking about it for the first time in this way could do no better than consult the experienced teachers of Art or Craft. For a long time, Art teachers, far from being the muddled other-worldly and fey creatures they were once thought to be (unless they affect this for purposes of enlisting sympathy), have had the most complicated responsibilities for space, materials and the requisitioning of supplies. As a breed they are quite remarkably able to master and then transcend this material organisation, so as to make their studies both efficient and exciting.

It is obvious that Art, Craft and Science specialists need to master their space and materials if they and their classes are not to be choked, either with paper or chemical fumes. But at the same time as their departments have become more complex, so too have those of the Humanities. Consider materials. The universal exercise book is now replaced or supplemented by a file or folder, for which loose paper, of various sizes and rulings, needs to be supplied. The standard textbook similarly must coexist with other printed material, either published or school-produced. Publishers now supply schools with kits involving single sheets or cards for individualised learning, or with sets of thirty copies of a single page for class discussion: teachers also make their own work sheets from rotary duplicators of increasing sophistication. It is much simpler to store, distribute, recover, check and return to store a set of thirty textbooks than to deploy a variety of books, cards, sheets and packs, and the muddle and expense can be appalling if the teacher has not mastered the techniques for doing it.

Printed resources are not the only ones in common use. We now make widespread use of tape recorders, film and film-strip projectors, record players and overhead projectors. Newer developments such as closed-circuit television and videotape recordings, are here and spreading. Each of these has its peculiar kinds of software, spools, strips, loops, discs, slides and cassettes, which the teacher must know how to obtain, conserve and use. What is more, he needs to enable his pupils increasingly to do these three things for themselves. They learn how to use them faster than their teachers, who are commonly rescued from technological distress, by young electronic wizards, but retrieval from store and conservation of supplies are skills the teacher just has to know and teach.

The development of all these kinds of materials has led departments, and now increasingly schools, or even groups of schools, to concentrate resources centrally. But just as the long existence of school libraries has not prevented the teacher from feeling the need also to have his own collection of books to hand, so teachers will continue to keep some stocks of other materials in the room as well as training pupils in the art of retrieval from the central resource bank.

Proliferation of hard-ware and soft-ware has led to increasing employment of non-teaching ancillaries. Local authorities will now usually make provision in their establishment for a school to have skilled aides. Until we are in a position to have an adequate supply of such help, schools at present have to decide just where they will put their few valuable ancillaries to greatest effect. A librarian, when a school is fortunate enough to have one (and every school needs one), cannot be expected to do any other job. But a skilled technician may be useful either as a laboratory assistant, workshop assistant or working entirely on supply and maintenance of audio-visual (AV) resources. In my own school for instance, Group 12 with 1,200 students, we have an establishment of eight laboratory and general assistants, besides the secretary, bursar and three clerical assistants.

So the teacher, far from being shut with his class into a classroom to spin everything out of his own head, needs to draw on all these resources. This is not just a matter of technical competence, though that is a part of it. Above all, in his modern, increasingly managerial role, the teacher needs to learn how to deal with people. In the past he could get by with knowing how to deal with boys and girls, with the result that he often could not deal with anybody else, or only if he could get away with treating them like schoolchildren—hence the stereotype quoted in Chapter 1, and why Mr Chips was infuriating to more people than he was endearing. 'A man amongst boys and a boy amongst men.' It is no use for a teacher to have a stores assistant, but never be on speaking terms with her, or a technical assistant who is lazy but whom he cannot encourage by methods other than hectoring empty threats. This is in addition to the managerial skill needed by teachers to organise visits by students out of school, to factory, office or theatre, and visits into school by members of the public with specialisms to offer. None of these arrangements can afford to be slipshod. Teachers are now having to employ the courtesies and stratagems that most other professions working in teams have found necessary. And a good thing too: it makes them seem less odd to their pupils.

It might be thought from all of this that a successful teacher is above all a skilled entrepreneur. I should hate to give such an impression. All this must be subservient to his concern for the growth through learning of the individual pupil. How far he needs to fight to keep this light burning amid all the draughts and gusts that could extinguish it may be seen from the following.

During a spell of comparative luxury in terms of time at my own disposal, I asked a young teacher, with his head's permission, if I might attach myself to him for one day in order to make careful note of everything he did. Our own memory is fallible and it is very difficult to monitor our own activity whilst engaged upon it. We were not strangers, as at the time I was supervising tutor to several students working with him and others in his department. I was therefore familiar to most of his pupils. The school was a large urban comprehensive, mixed sexes, 11–18, almost 50 per cent immigrants, new buildings. The teacher is a young married man, now a head of department elsewhere, but at the time last year, just a full-time assistant within a good English department. Call him Mike. I arranged to meet him in the car park on arrival on a Monday morning in early October.

8.45 Mike parks his car and immediately half a dozen kids are around him. He removes a 16mm projector from his boot. (Over the weekend he had been running through several films he was considering for school use.) Someone offers to carry the projector, but Mike explains that by rule he should carry it himself. Lets them carry spool-cans instead. He goes to the staffroom on the first floor, retrieves his films, thanks kids. He makes himself a cup of coffee at the staffroom counter and chats over it with his head of department and others. Head of department says she must have a minute at break to arrange times for students coming in from local college.

8.55 Mike crosses to his classroom (the nearest one to staffroom, which is perhaps a mixed blessing). He fetches exercise books from shelves to his desk. He unlocks a cupboard in which he stores stock for the book shop that he runs. A girl asks him to record a book sale.

9.0 Early arrivals drift in. Each has something to say to Mike, who listens and responds while continuing to check over his book stock.

9.10 Back across to staffroom where he collects mail from his pigeon-hole, and his class register.

9.15 Loudspeakers sound the pips for start of day (there is a public address loudspeaker in every room). Mike is in his room calling his register. His is a second year (12–13 year-olds). One girl hands him a letter from home explaining her absence last week. Mike thanks her, clips the note into his register and asks another girl why she has no note to explain her absence. The school secretary looks in. She needs a messenger: could Mike spare someone. A volunteer is sent off with her. Mike tells his whole class that at half-term he will be taking a party camping, that tomorrow he will have an official letter to hand out for them to take home. Two latecomers arrive and Mike repeats his announcement.

9.22 Mike lines them up inside his door, checks the corridor and leads them out to the hall for assembly. Today is Lower School assembly (1st–3rd years). Mike steers his class into rank, hushes a chatterer and checks that everyone can see a hymn book, as the monitor has given out a short ration. Form teachers stand down the side of the hall facing in towards their own class rank. Mike stays with his class to check in hymn books and see them off to first lesson.

9.45 Mike's first lesson, in his classroom. It runs without interruption.

11.0 Break. Mike collects coffee at counter. He finds head of department who now has up-to-date list of students due to start teaching practice at half-term. (A large school may take in students from at least six colleges, possibly each with different requirements.) They discuss which forms they might best place students with, which have been over-used, which might be risky until they know how assured the student is.

11.10 End of break. Back to classroom. Mike shares work this lesson with an assistant who is not an English specialist. (Half of the English taught in schools is in the hands of non-specialists. This school meets the problem by linking their specialists and non-specialists so that the specialist in a pair has direction of the work with the non-specialist as assistant.) Mike is therefore organising the work of two classes.

11.20 A remedial teacher enters. (She takes pupils needing attention to specific basic deficiences by a system of arranged extraction from other lessons. The trend is towards such an approach rather than one of more or less permanent segregation of those who show backwardness, which tends to label and then reduce them to 'dimmies'.) Because of absences, she explains to Mike, she has two unexpected vacancies. Could she have Jill and Barbara for some extra time? Mike agrees.

Some of the class are reading. Mike sends a girl to the library to borrow a book. She returns empty-handed to say the librarian refused to let her take one out as she has one overdue. Where is it? asks Mike. At home.

12.15 Mike sets homework. Desks, which have been clustered, are straightened up. Mike locks cupboards. He stays talking with some of the class who want to ask him about their work.

12.20 Mike goes to lunch. He sits, as do most staff, among pupils, chatting.

12.40 He returns to his classroom and sets up the daily book stall for sales. He is helped by two pupils and one probationer teacher, his regular assistants. Kids buying books talk to Mike and the assistant.

1.15 Bookstall is closed. Mike locks cupboard after helpers have put the stock away. Mike enters the sales in his records.

1.20 Afternoon registration. Mike reminds class that one month after the start of term he still has not had in the per capita contribution to school fund from everybody. He has to pay it in to the office by next week. Checks list, appeals to overdues, but gets nothing. He sends them off to lessons.

1.30 Third lesson. Fifth form. Mike adjusts his lesson plan to accommodate those who were absent last time into an on-going programme of work.

2.15 A discussion has developed with half the form and looks as though it may disturb the other half. Mike hastily searches locally for an empty room to which the debaters can hive off. There is none.

2.30 As the discussion reaches critical point, it is cut dead by a general announcement by the deputy head over the loudspeaker giving notice of a meeting of the school council.

2.35 End of lesson. Break with cup of tea in staffroom. Mike talks with a colleague who teaches English to another fifth form.

2.50 Fourth lesson. Fourth year class. Mike reads out a piece written by one of the class. A boy arrives late, so he starts again. A fresh interruption: two boys from Mike's own class enter and say they want their Maths books from their desks. Mike tells them to go away and next time to think ahead during afternoon registration.

There are not enough anthologies for one each. A check reveals that of those who took books home last week, six have failed to bring them back. This, Mike explains patiently to those who have objected, is why they must share.

3.10 A girl arrives late explaining that she has been at interview with a senior member of staff. This disturbs the poetry reading as she is dying to tell, and others to hear, what happened. She is in no mood to work and sits distracting others by puffing her bicycle pump.

3.50 End of school. Mike tells one boy who persistently disrupted the lesson, that he will have to report the matter to the fourth-year master.

Mike's class collect belongings from classroom. He has another word with the two who forgot their Maths books and sets them to help him tidy up the room.

Mike completes his teaching record for the day.

4.30 I take leave of Mike, as it has been exhausting enough for me just to watch him through a normal day. He remains marking books. I know that on other days by 4.15 he might be engaged on one of several other activities, such as a departmental meeting, a School Council meeting, a conference with the youth centre leader who is helping Mike organise the camping trip, mounting a display of work with pupils. I know also that one day that week he hoped to get away in time to buy a book on the way home.

I deliberately left out of this log any account of the content of the lessons. My purpose was to give a picture of the workaday conditions under which the teacher will arrange for teaching and learning. Lesson content is studied in research far more often than anyone considers the circumstances confronting the teacher.

On a different day I might have found that Mike had a play-ground patrol duty over his dinner hour, or a school play rehearsal. In the evening he might have visited a pupil's home. Schools vary widely in the extent of home visiting. Some schools discourage home visits, preferring parents to come to the school: some practise it extensively, knowing that it is just the parents that the teacher most needs to talk with who are the least likely to come for consultation at school. Where it is undertaken, parents, even those who are at first suspicious, appreciate the concern that obviously lies behind it. I have known cases where the first engagements were conducted through the letterbox of a front door that remained bolted, but where persistence brought understanding and co-operation. The teacher just needs to know his personal and professional limits though, so that the social worker can take over before role-inflation sets in.

Knowing Mike, it would not surprise me if that evening he had been called on by one or two of his pupils at his own home. It is an odd state of affairs if a teacher lives so far away from his school that he cannot be visited by his pupils. There are snags. In Jersey I was also called on from time to time by parents, usually farm-workers to whom I could not fairly say 'I shall be available at 9 o'clock tomorrow morning in school.' I even had one who thought I was persecuting him by putting an attendance officer on to him for keeping his boy home fishing: he called round in his old car with two or three Breton seasonal workers after they had all tanked up at the local. After coming twice when I was at school for the evening he gave up, which disappointed my eldest son who used to argue with him in the yard, but it relieved my wife.

Over a period of time teaching in a neighbourhood school, I have found that most of the shops and offices that I visit become staffed with ex-pupils, who are always able to give fresh news of their own friends and families. And there are the unexpected encounters that form a bonus: Alan, who raised a sparrow-hawk at school and who turns up tending the eagles at Gerald Durrell's zoo; the young men who buy you a drink when you have bumped into them in a pub; even Harry Briggs, whom I last met, vast, muscular, grimed with diesel oil, leaping across the dodge'ems on Blackheath Fair collecting fares, greeting me and family with, ' 'Ullo Mister Watts. Remember me? The worst boy in the school.' I suppose he was, but we had kept him on, which I don't think anyone else had ever done.

# CHAPTER FOUR

# Head Styles – School Styles

Now that you go to school, you will learn how we
call all sorts of things;
How we mar great works by our mean recital.
You will learn, for instance, that Head Monster is
not the gentleman's accepted title . . .

D. J. ENRIGHT

As recently as 1950 I told the mother of a good friend of mine that
I intended going into teaching. 'But John,' she said, 'doesn't that
mean you should take Holy Orders?' I assured her that this was
no longer necessary, even to become headmaster of Rugby,
which is what she may have had in mind. Still, it was my first
glimpse of a certain tradition of expectation of the schoolmaster,
and more particularly of the headmaster. At a time when the
power and status of the clergy has sunk almost below the horizon,
headmasters have been put into a position that enables them to
assume many of the priest's prerogatives, and indeed have been
expected to do so. As church attendance has declined over the
years of this century, the numbers of children in compulsory
school attendance has risen, thus transferring the congregation of
youth from vicar to head teacher.

Vicar and head at one time kept an equilibrium, but in time the
vicar dropped out of this power scene and the head held a com-

mensurately greater authority. It became priest-like because school days traditionally started with a service, and under the Education Act of 1944 it became obligatory for the day to open with assembly for an act of corporate worship. Although of late there has been a new emphasis on its being corporate, with the content and conduct of the assembly shared around staff and pupils, it has nearly always been part of the head's role to take the assembly. He, or she, determines its form, both liturgically and in spatial arrangement. The head is free to impose high ceremony and set prayers, or low order with improvised prayer. There is no bishop, congregational council or other special body to regulate the head teacher, as there would be for a priest, and his doctrine may be very cranky for all that can be done about it. In extreme cases, governors or the inspectorate would take action, but this is not their special province, so that no steps would be taken until some threshold of oddity had been crossed. Inside that boundary, the head can say and do what he pleases.

Morning assembly has always been the head's principal means of communication to the school, and indeed to the staff. It provides the head with a two-pronged fork since he starts with the religious service and then almost invariably continues with a secular part.

Of course, the religious presentation may emphasise the retribution and anguish of the Old Testament or the sweetness and light of the New, but either way round it will be received as from the same authority, the same agency, as will the later secular announcements. Regardless of whether the lessons are read by first formers or the hymns chosen by 4B this week, the message, broadly, is known to be the head's. Thus the head is seen to have, or be seeking to have, divine authority for his secular task. If from the same table, on the same platform, in the same assembly, and especially if from the same voice, school hears about Gideon scattering the host of Midian and then about prefects rounding up smokers in the toilets, an association is bound to be made as to whose side God is meant to be on. Not only has the head assumed the vicar's cassock, but the robes of the magistrate at the same time. And this can do things to a person.

It can do things to a person because it puts power into their hands to a degree that they may not even have expected, and from a position that is unlikely to have prepared them for it. A head is still given authority from above to run school more or less as he, or she, likes. 'Captain of the ship' is the much-worn metaphor employed, and as long as the ship keeps on course and unloads the goods expected by the shipowners, the authority of the captain is unquestioned. A sea captain has to obtain a master's certificate, which a head teacher does not, and it is not always possible to tell who is ready for headship. It is difficult to foretell how a person is going to respond to having power.

I doubt whether power invariably corrupts, though it certainly seems to change most people who acquire it. After all, power is the means to getting things done, and it would seem acceptable that anyone wanting to get things done should seek the necessary power to do so. It is however reasonable to ask what it is they want to get done, to whom they are accountable, and how that power is to be shared with others. As it is though, heads are appointed on a very broad brief, for an indefinite period up to retirement, are accountable nominally to their governors, and under no obligation to share power at all. This enables the inspired to be very effective. But the power remains even to those who are uninspired or whose inspiration is expired. They are the ones most at risk.

There are distinct occupational hazards in headship. One hazard is the realisation of a deeper-seated desire to play out some other authority role, to be in fantasy, if not in effect, either a vicar, or a psychiatrist, or demogogic politician. A little authority can go to the head and it is common to find that head teachers really believe that they are changing society, or on the other hand preventing society from changing, standing as moral bulwarks in an age of slipping standards. Mind you, in this delusion they are given ample encouragement from dozens of sources, each in their own way looking for some swift and simple solution to their own problems of fear and control. The head is asked nearly every day to 'do something', usually to say something in assembly, about this, that and the other of incredible diversity. He is one of the most accessible 'magic helpers' (to borrow a term from Eric Fromm), nearer to hand than the magistrate, the TV pontificator, the bishop or member of parliament. If only he will have a word with them about road safety, or behaviour in bus queues, or kindness to animals, or venereal diseases, or environmental protection, or the brotherhood of man with special reference to Asian immigrants, then somehow or other all would be well. It shows touching faith and is rather flattering, even if you have never harboured any pretensions to being a shaman. But it takes considerable courage and assurance to stand up to these demands, resist them, and face the consequent charge that it is because heads and their staffs are shirking their responsibilities that the country is plagued with violence, dental caries, non-biodegradable garbage and disrespectful shop assistants.

Even if the head resists these temptations there are still sizeable responsibilities to bear. He is answerable for the curriculum, the effectiveness of the teaching, the behaviour of the pupils, the care of the premises and the relationships with the outside world. The expectation of the school's pastoral responsibility has been so strong in England that I am often taken to task by members of the public over misdemeanours of my pupils in holiday periods well away from school. And to be fair, heads of selective schools have regularly claimed such authority, laying down such rules as when to go to bed and when not to visit the cinema. The head is even held responsible for the conduct of his staff: I have been asked by governors to check that one or two men smartened up their appearance and to stop another from serving petrol at a local garage during weekends as it tarnished the image of the school. The head, by implication, is expected to be a paragon of virtue.

Not surprisingly, comparatively healthy, sane and companion-

able men and women not infrequently undergo sad transforma-
tion under the strain when translated into headships. Certainly
they must expect a different set of relationships with the others on
staff from what they enjoyed as a fellow assistant. The head's
power determines so much of a teacher's working life that an
inordinate amount may come to depend on remaining in his good
books. He decides, with or without consultation, which forms
you are to teach, what share of the money available will be forthcoming to your department, what additional allowances shall be
added to your salary, what release you may have for in-service
courses and, perhaps most daunting of all, what is to be said about
you in report when you apply for another job. What he has not
got, in distinction from most other bosses, is the power of dismissal. Nevertheless, it is hardly surprising if under such circumstances, teachers treat their head teachers with caution and,
however far time and trust may soften it, reserve. Some will be
sure to say what they think the head wants to hear; some will
maintain their image of independence in the eyes of colleagues
by disagreeing with the head in public. Either way it is difficult
for the head to get an answer from staff by the question direct,
and heads often have to rely on the deputy to find out what staff
feel on a subject. But the sum total is unavoidable isolation in some
degree or other.

Isolation is a danger. Even the dedicated mystic traditionally
comes back eventually from the wilderness to share his visions,
but the head who has retired to a cloud seldom comes down—as
much as anything because he doesn't realise that he is on it. He
will be lucky to have a best friend to tell him, or it may be his
only way of avoiding a coronary, itself one of the most frequent
killers of heads. Three questions come to mind. Why become a
head? How can one survive it? Is the head really necessary?

Before answering these three questions it is worth looking at
what promotes teachers from their ranks to headship. The only
research into this (carried out recently by Gerald Bernbaum of
Leicester University's School of Education) has cleared up several

70

mysteries. For instance, heads represent much the same spread of class origin as all teachers, and are not appointed because of any social superiority in upbringing. They are better qualified, in terms of degree awards, than teachers in general, but less likely to have had any teacher training themselves. A third significant finding was that a far higher proportion of heads are Arts graduates, as distinct from mathematicians and scientists, than is found among graduate teachers as a whole. Whatever this tells us or does not tell us about the necessary qualities of a head, it tells us a lot about what those who appoint heads think is required of them. This is, a good academic qualification and an understanding of personal relationships. In spite of all that is being said currently about the need for a head to show managerial capability, of a kind one might expect of an economist, mathematician or scientist, what authorities and governors look for, and heads themselves advocate, is a capacity to handle people as people.

One becomes a head because it confers power, status and better pay than any assistant post. The other satisfactions that a teacher may achieve are there too, along with a sense of service and so on, but I don't know who would take on effective headship without being given power, money, and the status that goes with them. This is not as condemnatory as it may sound. Power is only to be condemned as an end in itself, otherwise it enables a person to say 'I know what needs to be done, how to get it done and am now in a position to get it done.' But the risks are great, personally, and warrant the danger money.

As for survival, there are one or two things I have learnt, though I must declare at once that a lot of my income still goes into life policies. To anyone contemplating headship I would first pass on to them the oldest piece of advice given to man: Know thyself. You need to know your own strengths and weaknesses and have checked your own insights against those of trustworthy colleagues while you can still be sure of an honest answer. If you wait to find out who you are until after taking up office, you may never discover more than the collection of masks that others have given you to wear. Then you may die the death of being all things to all men, with total loss of identity. So you need to know yourself well enough to examine your motives, to ask what it is you want to accomplish through the power that will be given you. How far, for instance, do you relish the thought of being able to tell old Buggins to shut up when he has been droning on at a staff meeting yet again? Or of telling Jenkins the Physics that he will just have to do as well as he can with a 50 per cent cut this year in his department's allocation?

Another key to survival, though it needs an odd blend of patience and discrimination, is to cultivate the art of listening. Perhaps as teachers we have all been too pleased with the sounds of our own voices. (At one stage at Les Quennevais, the teachers decided to eat separately from the children in another room. As a result they certainly had fewer interruptions to their arguments, but it was the children who remarked on the first day how nice and quiet it was at dinner time.) If we really want to know what people think, we have to listen, often for a long time. Heads have a tendency to tell a person what they believe that person is thinking, or at the best to accept the first thing that they are told when seeking an opinion. It is of course easy for most people to conceal facts, but given time to talk, relatively impossible to conceal attitudes. If you want to know a person's attitude to something all you need to do is learn to read the subtext (as linguists call reading between the lines) and then just listen for long enough. After that, considering all you do get told, you have to learn discretion, to a high degree.

Following from knowing oneself and knowing how to listen comes the need to judge other people. Although the teacher's position is becoming less isolated, it is still possible for him to work for the most part with children and to judge the rest of the adult world as a pack of fools, wolves in sheep's clothing or vice versa. He may need to be rescued from trouble with parents as a result, but he may still be an effective teacher even if he thinks every parish councillor a power-crazed fascist, or every salesman of educational technology an honest helpmate only hamstrung by the head's Scroogery. But a head with similar misjudgement of people from other walks of life can intensify the isolation for himself and the rest of the school when he should be relieving it. Above all, the head needs to seek out his allies and, when the time demands it, to confront his enemies. It is no use pretending that he won't have both: he desperately needs to know one from the other, and to distinguish from both of them the empty vessels whose noise he can safely disregard.

Every sane head that I know has been helped to stay that way by the life they make for themselves apart from the school, with friends and family. The head who is totally dedicated to the school (or indeed any teacher who is) becomes a menace to it. You need to be able to turn off, to stand back, and if necessary be forced to turn off. To do this there must be people about whom, or activities about which you can feel at least as passionately as you do about school. The danger signals need looking at very seriously if the yachtsman teacher finds he is failing to maintain the boat or the rose gardener is abandoning his shrubs to suckers and aphids. There is probably no better counter-irritant than one's own children of course. Not only do they distract you from worries, but they bring you off your high-horse. Unless the head's wife thinks he is a genius before whom all paths should be made smooth, all problems, including his own children, hushed up! Such a wife, by flattering the man's ego, should be impeached by his staff (and probably often is, if she knew it).

One last item in this small survival kit: a head should keep mobile. This opinion will be contested, but if it was true of Dr Arnold who had reformed Rugby and become restless by the age of forty, it is more true today at a time of infinitely increased rates of change: a head will have done his best for a school by the time he has been there for five years, and after ten years may well have become a liability. He needs fresh challenge to awaken his imagination, and he often needs to be taken off the hook of his own gaff, or gaffe. Ideally he needs breathing space to detach himself and examine his role.

But it is not easily done. Power is a golden ring which, as the saga-makers have always known, may be slipped on easily enough, but which grows increasingly difficult to remove. The withdrawal symptoms, as with other addictions, are painful. And then, although lip service is often paid now to the notion of mobility within the whole educational service, little is done to remove the obstacles, such as risk to salary and superannuation. Not all authorities pay removal allowances of any sort, and I have yet to hear of a teacher's displacement or resettlement allowance.

It is one thing to take such a step voluntarily, quite another to be required to do so. It could break a man to remove him forcibly from office, for no offence other than being ten years older than he was. Somehow, the humiliation must be taken out of it, possibly by heads becoming less exalted anyway in the future, and certainly by protecting salaries. Other professions too are looking for solutions to this problem of effecting dignified demotion. Perhaps in teaching it needs to become more general for heads in their fifties and sixties to take advisory posts, attached either to a local authority or, lightly loaded, to a school. (Only they will need to have learnt how to listen.)

Talking for too long about 'the head', I may have given the impression that heads are much of a muchness. They may on occasions show certain common identification marks, but there are many breeds and it may be worth distinguishing just a few by function if only because their way of functioning largely determines the nature of their schools and the conditions of life for their staffs. How does a head set about putting policy into practice?

He may rely on charisma, the power to persuade others by sheer presence, charm and strength of conviction. Some have immediate advantages in this respect, related perhaps to physical stature, assured manner, sweet reasonableness of the kind that hears out what you want to say but comes back with 'Nevertheless'. Or he may be a high-powered and tenacious arguer who

74

can leave most members of staff exhausted, not necessarily convinced but with no reply left so that they submit with resignation, perhaps admitting that he must know best. He will be about the school a lot, able to find the right word for the caretaker, the dinner ladies, as well as getting on well with his pupils. He will be a great taker-aside of teachers for the quick persuasive chat, and he will hold regular staff meetings since he is able to sway opinion by personal magnetism. He will have nothing to hide as he can always defend his actions or apologise convincingly for his mistakes. Staff will feel the security of knowing that he will go down well with governors and other committees, and with parents.

The main snag with charisma as a basis for leadership is that it fades. It is not enough if there is nothing more to it than power of character or power of speech; then people before long will see through it. It can degenerate into bluster and verbal bullying. If people don't respond to your sweet reasonableness after a while one can only assume that they are being obstinate, so you badger them instead. And the assurance that initially gave people confidence that he knew what he was doing, was aware of their problems and protecting their interests, can soon be reinterpreted as bland autocracy, especially if it becomes apparent that those problems and interests have been disregarded. So there needs to be something more there when the old magic fails.

One thing that needs to be there, with or without charisma, is administrative competence. We sometimes hear that a head today has become just an administrator. There is no need for this to happen. Admittedly, in a small primary school the head may be expected unfairly by his local authority to carry out clerical duties that will be time-consuming and distracting, but increasingly even schools of 100–200 pupils are receiving help, if only part-time, from clerical staff.

For the head, delegation is a necessity. Failure to delegate is the administrator's doom, and if a head fails to delegate but allows himself to be martyred behind a desk piled with papers then he is either incompetent or, more frequently I suspect, using it as a cover for the retreat that he has chosen to make from the personal contact with teachers and pupils. The competent autocrat may delegate the clerical work, clearing his desk of registers, returns and dinner accounts, but retain all the policy decisions himself. Charisma may or may not accompany it: it makes little difference in the long run if staff know that they have no say in basic matters of curriculum, discipline and the structure of responsibilities.

The competent autocrat will exercise his control by bureaucratic or hierarchical means, or a combination of the two. By bureaucratic control, the head may lay down all the routine procedures and maintain them by remote control. A lot will depend upon his communication system. He will issue many notes and have duplicated slips ready to cover all foreseen eventualities. I knew one who had hundreds of forms which saved him making personal contact. One read: 'Mr/Mrs/Miss...... I passed your classroom at .... a.m./p.m. today .... 19 .... and I noticed excessive noise. Would you please drop me a note of explanation.' He may give an appearance of personal touch by using a public address system, but the secret of the Tannoy is that it operates in one way only. No teacher who has taught as assistant for a few years with the threat of a loudspeaker introducing Big Brother unexpectedly every other lesson will ever want to use one, given the power to do so. Certainly I was inoculated against them.

If he can overcome the suspicion of his staff, the head may be able to draw them into a more democratic or collegiate participation in the running of the school. Some may suspect him of being weak and indecisive—'Why can't he make his mind up and get on with it instead of pestering us? Let us do our job, teach, and he do his.' But I think this kind of self-imposed limitation of collegiate responsibility is disappearing fast and I shall return to the subject in my last chapter. Suffice it to say here, that far from weakness or failure of leadership being the cause of participatory government in a school, it should spring from an altogether healthier concept of leadership. Where leadership derives from a wish to dominate others it is unhealthy. Domination, whether in the family, the classroom, staffroom (and for all I know, in the board room), stems from the possessive desire to control and consume others, to use them as means to one's own ends, as a justification of one's own supposed perfection. It is destructive and ultimately self-destructive. Leadership, in any real sense, can only operate at the point where there is no longer any desire to dominate others. Participation by staff in policy-making may be slow in getting off the ground, but teachers who have once felt the increased dignity of sharing this responsibility are very unlikely to abandon it again.

Which brings us to the last of my three questions about headship—is it really necessary? Whether the style of government is autocratic or consultative, the head normally makes the final decisions. At the autocratic end of the spectrum he will make them and either communicate them to the staff or let them play the well-known game of trying to discover what his policy is. At the other end, the head will consult staff opinion and will genuinely keep an open mind until he has heard all possible comment. Then he will decide. Staff will resent his consulting in the pretence of having an open mind if he has already made it up—this is only disguised autocracy. They are more likely to support his decision where they know that their opinion will count. Given this, they advise and consent.

A truly participatory government of a school is very rare indeed. Amongst independent schools it has been attempted successfully, as at the Rudolf Steiner schools and at Monkton Wyld school. Nowhere in England, even at A. S. Neill's Summerhill, is there a system of corporate staff-student government as there is in the experimental gymnasia (Forsøkgymnaset) of Norway, Sweden and Denmark. Within the maintained system of British schools we have gone further at Countesthorpe than anywhere else I know. Here the policy-making is in the hands of staff and, as far as they exercise their option, the students. The headship is therefore a peculiar one inasmuch as I have to carry out policies

77

that I am party to but which are not of my personal making. Thus the school is not the expression of my educational outlook, the outcome, within the usual constraints, of my will, as a head may normally expect to see himself identified by reflection in his school. Countesthorpe will never bear the stamp of my image.

Nevertheless, even in this situation the school needs internal co-ordination, executive stability and a public front runner. The head must see that matters are put on to agendas, that a schedule of deadlines is drawn up, that decision is reached, recorded and promulgated. He provides continuity and maintains the communications. He above all others (including the secretary and caretaker) must know what has happened, what is going to happen, and how those who need to are kept fully informed. Some one person is expected to be answerable to parents, local authority, governing body, press and public and there is no likelihood of a maintained school being established except with an appointed head, whether he is called Warden (as in the Cambridgeshire Village Colleges), Principal (as in our Leicestershire Community Colleges), or anything more fanciful such as Moderator, Chairman, or what you will. The time has not come, though it may well be on its way, when a local authority or board of governors will approve of a scheme for rotating school headships whereby staff nominate one of their own members to serve for a fixed term, say three years. It could of course provide one part of a solution to that problem of dignified demotion. In the meantime, I would stand by the answer I gave to a five-year-old son when I told him to come out from under the dinner table and he asked, 'Is a headmaster any better than a headache?' On balance, yes he is.

As things stand, then, the style of a school reflects its head, and the staff whom he appoints. (I deal more fully with methods of appointment in Chapter 6.) For that reason, I have dwelt at some length on heads and the variety of relationships teachers may have with them. But this variety of style can only operate within the organisation of schools determined by the local authority, the education committee of the elected council. Some brief description of the provision of different kinds of school is therefore called for.

I have concentrated my references on the publicly maintained school system because that is where 95 per cent of our boys and girls receive their education. (They are often loosely called 'state schools', which is erroneous since they are neither maintained nor controlled by the state.) The remainder attend independent fee-paying schools, mostly preparatory and soi-disant 'public' schools, give or take a few in the experimental fringe, and although it is one of the peculiarities of this country that these schools draw their clientele predominantly from families with wealth and power, their influence on educational thinking is negligible and their relevance to teaching in general merely vestigial, except for those who crave a comfortable bolt hole where 'it is a pleasure to teach small numbers of highly motivated children', as a teacher from Windlesham recently put it in a letter to *The Observer*.

Since the maintained system is not centrally controlled by the government, it does not present a uniform picture. Local authorities are charged under Act of Parliament to provide for the education of everyone in their district, and at present that includes, but is not confined to, those compelled to attend between the ages of five and sixteen. Even so, the provision is pretty generally divided into four levels: Infant 5–7, Primary (or Juniors) 7–11, Secondary 11–18, Further Education 16 upwards (full- and part-time).

Infant schools are frequently quite autonomous, though often run in conjunction with a junior school, each having its own head teacher. It is also increasingly common to find the one head teacher responsible for both infants and juniors. It is also becoming rare to find segregation of sexes at this level. Primary education is comprehensive, in that there is no selection; all children in a primary school's catchment area are eligible to attend unless they need the special provision made under the local authority for the handicapped. Primary schools vary in their internal organisation as this is determined by the head: the most contentious element in the organisation is the criterion used for making up the working groups of children. Nearly all divide them 'horizontally' into separate years, but whereas some divide them within the year according to interests, activities and friendship, others group them according to certain aspects of ability or performance. This latter practice is called 'streaming' and is the subject of much controversy.

The main cause of streaming in primary schools has been the system of selection for differentiated schools at the secondary level. Although several local authorities have introduced a level of Middle School 11–13 or 10–13 (with other variations), the age of transfer to secondary school is still generally eleven. This is the fracture point that gives its name to Eleven Plus, the procedure for dividing the ways into differentiated schools. It is a fracture point over which many children have been broken.

The history of our selective secondary school system can be read elsewhere. It is enough to say that the 1944 Education Act provided for the first time free secondary education for all. At that time it was thought advisable to make different provision according to ability and aptitude as shown against certain measurable standards between the ages of ten and eleven. Those who showed promise of high academic attainment, between 10 and 20 per cent, depending on local conditions, entered grammar schools. The bulk went to secondary modern schools, unless they joined the small elite at public and direct grant schools. There was also provision for those whose prognosis at ten years old suggested future technicians, by technical schools, but these never expanded and the system, though termed tripartite, has to all intents and purposes been clearly bipartite.

The system claimed a correspondence to a division by human nature into types—the academic, the technical, and the ordinary types—a ludicrously crude division of mankind if there ever was one. But it is no coincidence that it corresponded to the current analysis of occupations into manager, technician, and worker, in roughly the right proportion. Forecasts at ten years old are valid mainly as self-fulfilling prophecies. It was soon clear that those who went to grammar school soon displayed 'grammar school' characteristics, while those at secondary modern schools under-achieved because they arrived with a clear sense of having failed. Furthermore, there was a massive built-in class discrimination. One check* showed that from children of a given measurable level of intelligence (IQ 120), only 12 per cent of those from working-class homes 'passed' for grammar school, while 46 per cent of those from middle-class homes did. And so we found ourselves with a bipartite system that hardened the main class division as sharply as the distinction between officers and men in the forces.

It is against this division that we must view the emergence of the comprehensive school, the support for their growth and also the resistance to them. A comprehensive school is, like a primary school, simply one which takes in all the children from its area; they come together from the contributory junior schools instead of being sent to either the school for sheep or the school for goats. In 1958 there were about 100 comprehensive schools in existence: by 1970 they had grown in number to more than 1,000 and of 3 million pupils in secondary schooling 606,000, that is, nearly a fifth, were attending them. It should be pointed out, of course, that many of these schools are comprehensive only in name since they are not taking in all the children from their primary schools: some are still going to grammar schools. As long as there is any selection at eleven there can be no comprehensive school, only an enlarged and perhaps minimally enriched secondary modern. To claim otherwise, or to suggest as some politicians do that comprehensives can and should coexist peacefully with grammar schools is hypocritical double-think and parents should not be deceived.

There is no definitive kind of comprehensive school. Given the basic requirement of non-selective intake, there are varieties in the age range covered, in size and in internal organisation. A

* J. W. B. Douglas, *All Our Future* (1968)

comprehensive school may divide its intake into numerous streams. The early comprehensives in the 1950s tended to do this, continuing in many respects the selective and divisive process of the bipartite system. Though removing the stigma attached to being in a failures' school, it depended too heavily on the low-stream pupil feeling a compensatory sense of belonging to a high-prestige school. This was not satisfactory though and the tendency over the last decade has been towards both smaller comprehensive schools (ie under, rather than over, 1,500 pupils) and towards mixed-ability groupings.

In some comprehensive reorganisation, three tiers have been established, as in Leicestershire where Primary is 5–11, High School 11–13, and Upper School 14–18. In one or two areas such as Southampton, the students over sixteen are concentrated in a Sixth Form College which replaces the sixth forms of the contributory schools. The Sixth Form College has been one solution to the drift away from grammar and comprehensive schools by some students at sixteen who do not so much want to stop studying but want to leave school. These particular early-leavers have seen sixth form merely as staying on at school, especially if there are still restrictions and regulations regarding dress and appearance, or monitorial duties to be carried out. They tend to enrol then at a College of Further Education where they may study for what exams they please and regulate their own time and appearance as they please. Principals of Colleges of FE and heads of grammar schools have consequently found themselves in embarrassing rivalry at times, but I know of instances of regulations for sixth formers being considerably modified as a result of the students voting with their feet.

At this point it is worth noting that the extent to which the head and staff feel it incumbent upon them to regulate these minutiae of dress and manner will affect not only the attitude of their students to the school but also the kind of teacher who will want to work in it. Hardly a day passes without a newspaper publishing some story of a head's demands upon the personal lives of pupils or parents, with the action appearing in an absurd light. Apologists for the head's rights to make such demands will say that the press slant such stories so that they are made to look absurd, that the reasonable can be made to seem unreasonable. It is true that 'head-bashing' is an attractive sport, if only because so many in a position to indulge in it need to retaliate for humiliations and injustices suffered in their own school days: the sins of our pedagogical fathers are regularly visited upon us, their children! But even allowing for that, the mere facts of so many cases speak for themselves. 'A headmaster who has sent a brother and his sister home from school nine times for wearing gaudy pullovers agreed yesterday that he is colour blind.' This very day, as I sit writing this, my paper reports a headmaster who 'has ruled that upper school girls may not wear ponchos, ankle-length skirts or smocks during school hours when the rest of the pupils wear uniform'. Another head I knew boasted of a case that became known in the press as 'the battle of the thin red line' because he had suspended a girl for insisting on wearing a jumper which infringed the regulation grey by having a thin red line round the bottom of it. Her mother had knitted it, but, by jingo, he had stood his ground in the face of public outcry and won. I could only feel that, quite apart from the sheer effrontery of expecting the girl to discard her mother's gift and work, the whole thing was an enormous waste of valuable time and effort that should have been deployed on the real issues that any school has crying out for attention.

School uniforms are poor value for money, as a little consumer research will show, and yet one of the arguments advanced in support of uniform is that they prevent children's demands for expensive fancy clothes. The only expensive fancy clothes that I see in schools *are* the uniforms. Having started a school with no uniform I have witnessed that children and their parents experience no difficulty in finding clothes appropriate to school work, that class differences are not demonstrated by the costliness of clothes, though they may well be by styles. The advocates say it looks nicer, or smarter, or gives a pride in belonging. The demand usually persists when these arguments are demolished, because they are not the real and deeply felt causes for the demands.

Teachers and parents who want uniforms are really looking for what is the most immediate and recognisable symbol of control in a school. This is the real issue: that uniform is the outward show of a particular kind of discipline. It happens however to be part of a discipline that is no longer appropriate. Discipline is often spoken of as if it existed in its own right, like cod liver oil, to be administered when necessary. The truth is that discipline is a function of learning. If the style of teaching and learning is modelled on mechanical instruction, such as a sergeant gives in arms drill, then his style of discipline will be appropriate. It rules out individualised response: to be correct all the responses must be identical. Teaching used to be much closer to this model than it has become, and uniform was symbolic of that style and discipline. Of course, if the teacher's attitude to his pupil is still based on a belief in 'moulding character', making them grow in conformity to a given pattern, and in the efficacy of imparting the knowledge that he decides they should have, then the discipline of obedience, reverence, conformity will be appropriate, and so will uniform. But if, as we have steadily come to realise, teaching entails not domination, but the guidance of individuals as they grow, each in a different and unforeseeable way, and learning occurs best within a trusting relationship between teacher and student, then a different discipline is appropriate and it is not likely to include school uniform. Along with the use of corporal punishment, school uniform is a peculiarly British foible, but good as we are at fighting rearguard actions, I expect both of these features to disappear within a few years.

This is not an argument for uniformity between schools. Diversity, the right to be different, is a British foible that I find admirable. But the differences will continue to be differences of style as much as differences in basic organisation. There is no such thing as *the* grammar school or *the* comprehensive school. Each

84

school, being a community of people, will take on their communal characteristics, and no two will be identical. Parents, inasmuch as they have any choice of school, or, having sent their child to one, have any means of affecting what happens in it, will want to know what are that school's characteristics, and how those in it, staff and students, determine those characteristics. To refer back to Miroslav Holub, he did not mean headteachers when he wrote

> There is much promise
> in the circumstance
> that so many people have heads.

# CHAPTER FIVE

# School and the Public

As a boy I liked the story in my Latin book of the schoolmaster in a beseiged city who sought to win favour from the beseiging forces by bringing out to them the sons of his leading patricians, all pupils of his. They unsuspectingly accompanied their treacherous teacher on what was probably thought to be a harmless 'nature walk' and found themselves offered up as political hostages. But, the story goes, the general being a man of honour refused to stoop to such low practice, was disgusted by the schoolmaster's unprofessional behaviour in fact, and arming each boy with a rod, told them to drive him back home before them, making sure that he got a good taste of his own medicine. The story was recorded without a moral, though each reader can invent his own. It could be seen to imply that teaching and politics don't mix.

Today, the high proportion of MPs who were formerly teachers testifies to a more successful transition being possible. But it has always been a pitfall for teachers that they can become isolated in the classroom from the realities of the world, confined as they are to contact with the young and inexperienced, preoccupied as teachers can be with the past. Of course, if such isolation remains unbroken it will have adverse effects on the teaching. The young are more concerned with the future than the past, if only because they have got more of it, and an isolated teacher contemplating the future is too easily prone to idealism untempered with experience. As Alvin Toffler was recently quoted as saying, students 'have a right and a responsibility to ask teachers what a course has to do with their personal future'. So the teacher is under an obligation to take steps to see to it that he engages positively with the world outside the classroom, and by doing so continuously, rather than in fits and starts, to do so with less naïveté than the Etruscan schoolmaster of the story.

Unless the teacher chooses the dead-end of isolation, he will exploit the more obvious contacts that will keep him alert to the run of normal life, parents, local employment, other people through their interests and activities whether in clubs or informal groupings ranging from golf players to poetry readers. He will find increasingly today that school teaching means contact with the social services, with probation officers and youth workers. But it is probably as well to take up at this point the constitutional links between school and public through the employing authority and governing body, even if these are not the channels through which the teacher is likely to find that necessary regular concourse with the world of reality.

Every local government authority is required by Act of Parliament to provide for the education of the people in their district. It is worth noting that this is a far wider brief than merely to maintain schooling for those in full-time compulsory education. It extends to provision of further education for those who have left school and need to continue with training and qualification either in their spare time or on part-time release from employment, so that most local authorities now support Colleges of Further Education. It covers provision for Adult Education, which differs from FE in that it caters principally for those activities that people *want* to follow or learn more about for their own personal satisfaction, rather than for any vocational advantage. This is often organised through institutes which operate in the evenings at the authority's own primary and secondary schools, with a quite distinct staffing from the day school. Then

87

there are the obligations to cover special needs at schools for the handicapped and subnormal. Authorities vary in the provision made for nursery schooling since their legal obligation only extends down to the five-year-old. The likelihood is at the moment that the government will stretch the obligation down to the under-fives so that practice will become more consistent between authorities. All these services entail the employment of teachers.

A local authority will establish and maintain the schools, colleges and institutes that cover this service through its Education Committee and its permanent officers. The Education Committee will consist of elected members of the local council. The permanent officials of the Education Department will be local government officers headed by an appointed Director of Education. A county or a city Director of Education is a man with far-reaching power over the form of schooling open to the young of his area, and the conditions of work for the teachers in it. He advises the Education Committee, prepares their forward planning, informs them of current situations, and provides their regular key to what the government's Department of Education and Science is up to. The education service of a locality will inevitably carry the mark of its Director, but his powers will have been moderated by the need always to win the support of the Education Committee and council. He needs therefore to have vision and imagination not only in understanding educational needs, but also in handling committees.

It may be that the offices of Directors of Education are now being filled increasingly by more self-effacing 'systems men', men who know the machine through which they have risen and can operate it without dominating it. They correspond in some respects to the headmasters who operate a delegatory or hierarchical school and depend less than in the past on the personal charisma that made a one-man show possible. It may be that the increased complexity of any local service, and the attendant proliferation of specialisms within it, while making a more precise provision possible, is at the same time rendering it more cumbersome, less open to change, less likely to be any one man's instrument. For better or for worse we may not for a long while again see local education authorities identified with the name of one man, as was Cambridgeshire's with Henry Morris (retired 1956), Leicestershire's with Stuart Mason (retired 1971) and the West Riding of Yorkshire's with Sir Alec Clegg.

The Director is responsible for recommending the most appropriate form of school system for his district and must therefore be able to fuse the fullest educational thought, theory grounded in research, with knowledge of practical realities in terms of local politics and finance. Over a period of time, with the inevitable comings and goings of elected council members, an adroit Director could acquire extensive power and status. He needed it if he was to carry through reform or innovation of any size, as with Henry Morris's establishment of the Village Colleges, or Stuart Mason's reorganisation of Leicestershire into its three-tier comprehensive system.

The power could go to the head, as it did with Henry Morris, who in his last years in office behaved towards teachers and children as if they were at best puppets on his strings, and puppets made only by 'nature's journeymen', while at the worst they were intruders into the finished creations of his chosen architects. This was at a stage of his career when all 'his' schools were under the charge of 'his' appointed heads and it was no doubt difficult for him to take less than a baronial attitude towards it all. I was a young teacher under his authority in those last years and we lived in fear of him. He was unpredictable, hawk-like in his visitations and merciless in his wrath if his eye was offended. The word would go round Sawston—'Henry is on his way out!' The fountain would be turned on and the cast-iron animals that stood sentinel at the ornamental front doors would be hurriedly brushed and oiled. He once arrived unannounced on a summer evening while I was rehearsing a scene from *The Winter's Tale* on the fountain lawn. I felt rather proud of this—children staying after school rehearsing, while in one corner of the lawn was the choir singing 'When Daffodils Begin to Peer' in a setting specially written for them by Margaret Wander, their choirmistress. Surely the great man, suddenly appearing at the front of the lawn would take this in at a glance and commend it with warmth. Not a bit of it. What he saw was that Margaret, to conduct her choir, was standing on one of his four precious marble balls that rested one at each corner of the lawn. Morris flew into a rage and shouted at Margaret to get off. The singing faded and in horrified silence the children heard how those balls had been transported at his own expense all the way from Italy. The choir adored Margaret and afterwards asked me fiercely who that horrid old man had been.

It is sad to think that those and other children, who today are parents with their own children in Henry Morris's Village Colleges, may only remember him as an unreasonable and unkind old man, and that there are many teachers who will only have seen that darker side of his passionate care for school environment and for the work of artists and craftsmen that he placed around us. It is sad because Morris was one of those rare men who had an idealistic vision which he then, against all opposition, went ahead and put into practice. He was also the man who said so prophetically 'When I speak of the extension of education, I don't mean the extension of formal education by instruction and discourse, I am thinking of the effective organisation of communal living.'

Education authorities vary in the degree to which they delegate the appointment of teachers. It is general for them to maintain the fabric of their school service by taking a major hand in the appointment of head teachers, after which the decisions are left to the head teacher and the governing body. The authority will establish a governing body, or board of management, for each school by appointing a balanced number of nominations from the political parties and from district councils. The articles of government laid down for a governing body will provide a constitution including the representation in its membership. Usually the local university's Institute of Education will be invited to nominate one of its staff as a governor. There will be powers of co-option, and following the lead given by the Inner London Education Authority in 1971, many authorities are now encouraging boards of governors and managers to appoint one or two parents to membership. Also on the increase is the practice of one or two tteachers being invited to attend governors' meetings, though usually without voting rights. In Sheffield, governing bodies have been empowered to co-opt senior school students into membership.

Governors are responsible technically for the maintenance of sites and buildings, and for curriculum and discipline within the school. Normally they concentrate on the first and delegate the rest to the head teacher and staff, continuing to exercise influence by making staff appointments and by gracing school with their presence from time to time at functions. In practice even appointments are often delegated to the head, with perhaps the chairman of governors or a small subcommittee there for consultation. With the growth of the local authority's official staff machine, which undertakes maintenance by direct arrangement with the school head, the function of a governing body becomes even more nebulous, since there is no one specific matter for which it has real and sole responsibility. It sometimes appears like a watch-dog and at others like a jelly-fish.

As the watch-dog, the governing body may monitor the school on behalf of the local public, asking awkward or helpful questions for the public, of the staff, or more particularly of the head; and it may defend or publicise the school to the public, supporting the staff and head when criticised or neglected. As the jelly-fish it may be stranded without a role, embarrassed by appearing to patronise in an age that scorns patronage, or filling a platform at functions such as speech days while such formalities are steadily dropping out of practice. As teachers increasingly give time to establishing direct contact with school parents, so they tend to feel that their governors are unrepresentative of the public they are meeting and may very often have expectations of the school in conflict with the interests of most of the students in it.

The relationship of head teacher to chairman of the governors is somewhat akin to that of Director of Education to chairman of the Education Committee. One is the professional adviser and executive, the other is the interested lay man, the public's representative, the man or woman of public affairs. It would be a most foolish head or director who failed to acknowledge what he stood to learn from his chairman. Above all he learns what the public locally will stand for and what they are beginning to rumble about. The chairman is both barometer and seismograph from whom the professional can judge his essential timing. The good chairman knows what to trust to professional delegation and what to offer advice on, if the head has not had the sense to ask it already. My present chairman is a doctor who has said to me when meeting candidates for a teaching post, 'I would not presume to say which would be the ablest teacher any more than I would expect you to know who would best be my new junior partner, but I can offer an opinion, as a parent and as one who meets many people, on how they strike me as persons.' And I value that opinion.

In the small district of Jersey I was able as headmaster to share a rather unusual professional relationship with my Director, Charles Wimberley, and with the president of the Education Committee, Senator John Le Marquand, who was also my chairman of governors. They made an extraordinary pair those two— the one a courteous, scholarly, modest, patient and painstaking administrator; the other an ebullient, demonstrative, emotional and intriguing politican. Wimberley was a private man and Le Marquand a public figure. You couldn't find a more contrasted pair, and yet their effectiveness lay in their shared passionate conviction that greater justice needed to be done by the majority of the island's children. Jersey is socially more stratified and resistant to change than its own granite is geologically, yet those two brought change steadily about.

I doubt whether many people really knew the Director, though he was a familiar figure, especially around the schools. Some thought him indecisive when in truth he was considerate of people, never pushing a scheme, however attractive in the office, if it was likely to damage teachers or children. Your Jerseyman sees life more as Goethe did, with each man being either the hammer or the anvil: Charles Wimberley was often misunderstood because he nudged things forward in a more humane manner. When he came to Jersey, well after the war, elementary school-children were still being made to stand and literally to tug the forelock when the Director entered a classroom. Jersey underwent none of the social upsurges that the war brought to Britain. In 1945 after the Germans left, it at first just carried on where it had left off, which was as a hierarchical community verging on the feudal. In many respects, and certainly in the notion of popular education (though I suspect not in matters of banking and accountancy), they were twenty years delayed in their thinking. Charles Wimberley had to sow the idea of secondary education for all and then steadily bring it into reality: he certainly did not find many crying out for it, since they did not know what it was. Another instance of someone having to lead the prisoners out of the cave that they might see. Although he brought the education service from being twenty years out of date to well less than ten, he had not had to hustle people. Towards the end of his career there he said to me in response to some impatient remark, 'The tide is rising and there's no need to take a broom to sweep it in.'

John Le Marquand on the other hand was known to thousands, really known, not just as a political persona. People might have hated him, he was not afraid of incurring hostility, but I observed only a small number of private jealousies of his success, and otherwise an enormous public love of the man among ordinary people. I once travelled back from Guernsey on the boat with him after some meeting and in the course of a two-hour journey I should think over half the passengers walking by our seats greeted him as an old friend, shared a joke with him about some event out of their past, answered his inquiries about their relatives and went away heartened. He never patronised, he knew their way of life, shared it, loved it. Mind you, he knew how to get his own way, when to plead and when to bluster in the States (Jersey's Assembly). He never suffered pretentious fools for long, always did his homework (or at least made sure that his officers did it in time for him), taught me to do the same when bargaining for school money with businessmen on committees, when to engage in battle and when, like General Kutusov (another of my heroes) to avoid it. Once his mind was made up he could be quite maddeningly stubborn: there were times when he infuriated me, as when in the face of all apparent reason he refused, in spite of our parents undertaking to cover the costs, to agree to our having our swimming pool heated. At times like that he would simply avoid seeing me for a week or two until I had simmered down. Then there was some other urgent issue to settle, and he would suddenly lance that earlier sore by jokingly letting out, 'I've just visited two Guernsey schools with heated swimming pools: don't know how those blighters manage it!' One knew that he was adamant, the subject was closed, but the conflict had left no ill feeling. He knew the children in my school, he knew their parents and their grandparents. In a way he belonged to the age of paternalism from which he himself was pushing and dragging them towards greater self-respect. But unlike most of his powerful contemporaries he caused those whom he helped to feel more human and more dignified, rather than less. He was a man of clear, simple principle, whatever the political in-fighting he engaged in. At a time when we are moving into huge uncertainties it is helpful to identify a man like John Le Marquand who could keep his own faith bright while continuing to delight in the young and the adventurous. And he was fun.

From others who have been elected into a little local power you can learn sharply of common attitudes that might otherwise be concealed or softened for you. There was the bouncy committee man who breezed into my room on his first visit to the school, looked quickly round and then burst out 'Well, where's your cane, headmaster? Where is it? When I was a boy, our old head kept his on his desk. Could see it as soon as we entered the room. Never forgot that.' Very jocular, he was, but obviously saying what many a reticent parent had been thinking as they first sat in my room.

It is probably even instructive to have on a governing board someone who is obdurately ignorant of what the system is attempting to achieve so that they can say the maddening and misinformed things that others will undoubtedly be saying to each other, but not voicing to the teachers. Like the visiting governor of a comprehensive school who said 'It would be so much nicer for you all here if you did not have to take in the awful children from the estate', thereby revealing a total failure to grasp the idea of comprehensive non-selection.

What contact does the assistant teacher have with these other people, drawn from quite different walks of life, from which so much can be learnt about the world as it is? Certainly not as much unavoidable contact as the head teacher, who usually has more time in which to be available to visitors. Still, school has become increasingly open to visitors, and parents in particular. Notices at the gate saying 'Parents must wait here', are now disappearing, though as long as there are cases of burly fathers walking in and assaulting the teacher there will be districts where teachers will restrict completely open house.

Our educational system has hardly yet emerged from its initial stage of division between those schools where parents felt sufficient identity of aims with the teachers to leave them to get on with the job, and those schools where parents could see little such identity, regarded school still as an imposition from above, and were therefore in conflict with teachers as a stock class enemy. Either way round, the teacher minimised parent contact, whether because he was trusted or because he was mistrusted, it came to the same thing. The middle-class parent with middle-class teachers felt safe; the working-class parents of children in pre-

95

dominantly working-class schools, even with middle-class teachers, might feel suspicious but at least had a community of interest with fellow parents; the parents who suffered most were either middle-class parents whose children were at secondary modern schools and feared that working-class values or habits would debase their sons or daughters in spite of middle-class teachers (hence the strong support for streaming which would at least tend to keep together children of like interests), and most alienated of all, parents of working-class children who went to grammar schools. (A study by Jackson and Marsden, *Education and the Working Class*, a very readable paperback, makes their bafflement abundantly clear.)

It has only been with the rise of comprehensive schooling, first in the primary schools as middle-class parents began to entrust their young to a common mix, and now increasingly at the secondary level, that we find parents both wanting to voice their queries, doubts or demands and having the confidence and ability to do so. Under these circumstances, teachers have increasingly given time and thought to explaining their work to parents and to discussing the individual child's progress. It is no longer enough for parents to feel that they will learn all they need to know from the speeches at annual prize day plus a termly report. These more formal and unidirectional communications are being replaced by a more continuous dialogue.

Some schools prefer to keep these exchanges individualised, with maximum possibility of parent meeting those who teach their child. Increasingly, though, schools have formed Parent-Teacher Associations or Parents' Associations in a spirit of co-operation, to foster good relationships and to induce the more reserved parents to take the opportunities of meeting teachers, and each other. There is always the danger that the PTA and its committee will be dominated by the articulate committee-minded parents, who will tend to be middle class, oriented to sherry or coffee party contact, who will unwittingly drive out the working-class parents who in this country today are still largely unused to organising themselves in protection of their own interests. This is one reason why some heads refuse to form a PTA, though the more frequent one is that it will form a pressure group that will attempt to influence the way the school is run. This may be the truth.

Even if it is, it is pusillanimous to refuse parental requests for association in a body. The head still has more than adequate safeguards for his, or his staff's determination of the conduct and curriculum of the school. At times he expresses fear of parents taking over as they do in the United States. The fear is unreasonable. In the States, parents can heavily influence the local School Board, and thereby the appointment of head and staff, which it makes. The School Board, unlike our own Education Committee, consists of members chosen directly for it by local public election. It determines what money is available and can therefore control curriculum. In this country, the teachers have a degree of autonomy in curriculum unknown to their fellows in the States. In my own experience I have found parents ready to accept a constitution which is suggested as standard by the Federation of PTAs and which includes a clause stating that the determination of conduct and curriculum is the headmaster's. This of course leaves it wide open for parents to advise and argue, but this is very different from their controlling. And it is really very narrow and arrogant of teachers if they close their ears to parental advice and argument. Of course a head could find a totally hostile parent body battering at his door, but there must be something wrong if that happens, and he ought not to bury his head. Anyway, that should be a rare situation, since only a small minority of parents could really be so perverse as to knock the school in which their own children are, and on whose success and good name they depend. There are such, but the joy of a PTA is that they can usually be put in their place by the common sense of the majority: as often as not in any group discussion, I have found that in the face of attack from an unreasonable critic my defence and argument for the school has been taken over by supportive parents. In forming a PTA a head will usually find that far from playing into the hands of opponents, he is mobilising his supporters.

The press and television have helped change the image of the teacher, or at least caused the teacher to change it himself. The increased publicity given to teaching has helped to show that the schoolmistress is seldom a dowdy old schoolmarm and that any schoolmasters who still care to appear as bumbling old recluses have only themselves to blame if their notions seem removed from reality. The very fact that anyone may be reading this book, which is not being written for teachers, is another small indication of public interest, through the media, in education.

This raises the question of who should determine the curriculum. If the teachers are fully professional, should not the curriculum be for them and them alone to determine? Or are there wise and informed voices from society at large which should be heard in any curriculum-making? One way to look at it is to separate the appraisal of a curriculum for effectiveness from the appraisal of its validity. The first job, seeing that the objectives are being pursued in the most efficient way, can then be viewed as a professional task, calling for expertise and experience from the teachers. The validation would be a critique of the objectives against both the needs of society and the needs of human beings: since these two sets of needs may be in conflict, the validation will be highly contentious, calling for the wisdom of philosophers and not just the opinions of politicians in power.

Parents, given this division of juries deciding what should go on in schools, have a right to a voice in validating objectives, but should not be given the free run that some demand. Children, particularly adolescents, often need protection from the demands of their parents. The law recognises that, though it usually speaks in terms of physical violence rather than of psychological domination. Therefore any consensus of parents, however such an elusive oracle is to be conjured, must be taken as only one factor in the determination of curriculum objectives. Parents don't always know what is best for their children, bitter as that pill may be to swallow. And before the cries of protest rise up against the submission of ordinary people to the monstrous regiment of experts, let us consider that with all adolescents staying at school until 16, and an increasing proportion staying until 17, 18 or 19, the people who ought by all rights to have an increased voice in shaping the curriculum are the students who are themselves being subjected to it. This is not to suggest that the fifteen-year-old be allowed to do what he or she likes at school, with licence to do anything or nothing. It is requiring students to engage with their peers and seniors in the world at large to see what their present and future needs (ie objectives) are, and to engage with teachers in determining what studies and attitudes are presently necessary to achieve those goals. Looked at in this way, the student is the key figure, the one able to span the external validation of curriculum and the internal means of effecting it.

Even given a decent set of objectives for a school, who will devise the structures and programmes (or to use the commoner parlance, curriculum and discipline) to fit the bill? More particularly, who will promote the innovations needed to change a school when it is no longer meeting the needs of its students? Management theory suggests that impetus for change needs to come from outside the system it is to affect. Daniel E. Griffiths formulated a number of propositions about change that have come to be used commonly in reference to innovation in schools. These include the contentions that 'the major impetus for change in an organisation comes from the outside', 'change in an organisation is more probable if the successor to the Principal is from outside the organisation than if he is from inside', 'when a change in organisation does occur, it will occur from the top down, and not from the bottom up', and 'the more hierarchical the structure of an organisation, the less is the possibility of change'.

If one accepts all this, as I do basically of schools as they are almost invariably structured at present, one of two things needs to be happening. Either the country must make sure that responsible and competent agencies exert influences for changes in school from without, or else schools need to be restructured internally so that change may be expected from within. The second, more professional development is one I shall explore in the final chapter. It is a possibility that is still a long way off. In the meantime, the external agencies exist and operate.

The longest standing direct influence brought to bear upon teachers is that of Her Majesty's Inspectorate. Operating from the Department of Education and Science, they cover the country on a regional basis, observing, reporting and advising. They report to school governors and local authorities, but more particularly to the government in the person of the Secretary of State for Education and Science (formerly Minister of Education), and they advise teachers and head teachers. They are for the most part men and women who have themselves taught, and though most of them advise mainly on their own special subject, all have a general care and are expected to display mature powers of judgement in educational matters. Occasionally Her Majesty's Inspectors gang up and subject a school to a General Inspection. This is an anxious time when heads announce their rejection of the deplorable 'tendency towards window-dressing for HMIs' and then furiously revise records, call for all departmental schemes of work to be updated, stiffen the discipline and release moneys for extra-curricular activities.

Stories about HMIs are legion, but I shall not repeat any as I believe they are all apocryphal, invented by teachers as a means of self-defence against a genus whose power they fear. I have seldom known of an HMI doing any harm, but he lodges in the gullet of the teachers' racial memory from the era of the early Board Schools when salaries were determined annually on the outcome of the Inspector's visit to test the progress of pupils. 'Payment by results' was a shameful system, leading to shameful abuses, and its shadow even now darkens the relationship between the classroom teacher and the HMI who appears very occasionally and can be a valuable consultant.

The limitation of the Inspectorate as a force for change within schools arises from their own lack of resources and specific joint project proposals. A much more potent agency came into existence with the creation in 1964 of the Schools Council. It was established by the DES to review and reform curriculum and examinations. Its precise terms of reference were:

> . . . to uphold and interpret the principle that each school should have the fullest possible measure of responsibility for its own work, with its own curriculum and teaching method based on the needs of its own pupils and evolved by its own staff; and to seek, through co-operative study of common problems, to assist all who have individual or joint responsibilities for, or in connection with the schools' curricula and examinations to co-ordinate their actions in harmony with this principle.

Control of the Schools Council is in the hands of those working in the educational service: teachers, inspectors, local authorities, universities. Their work has included these main activities: issuing pamphlets and working papers of suggestions for curriculum development; urging local authorities, successfully, to set up Teachers' Centres where staff from the schools in an area can meet and organise new teaching approaches and materials between themselves; setting up research and development projects; publishing materials produced by these projects; advocating production of technological equipment found necessary by teachers for their developments.

There can be no doubt at all about the impetus towards change that the Schools Council has had upon thinking and practice in schools, but since its brief opened with that very clear caveat about upholding the autonomy of the school in determining its curriculum and method, in many schools the effect has been only to harden reaction. The more likely force for change within schools that pride themselves on hard-headed realism and a disregard for airy-fairy novelties (or whatever it is that they see the Schools Council holding out to them), will be the employers. Employers form a body that exerts pressure on schools, often through parents.

On a national scale, and looking forward to the requirements in employment over the years ahead, the demands of employers should contribute a positive influence over the validation of curriculum. If it worked in that way, we might well hear how our survival and prosperity is going to depend on 'a body of citizens who can make responsible choices with less support than in the past from precedent, tradition and dogma' (to quote Derek Morrell), how society is going to need increasingly the qualities of inventiveness, initiative, adaptability and a readiness to solve problems. This should indeed be built into the objectives of any school curriculum and more power to the world of employment if it can exert the necessary influence.

But it is more often nothing like this that the school is made to feel. Far from the considered view of anyone who has thought out a prognosis for employment over the coming two decades of the century, what the school is likely to hear is the immediate and short-term demand of the employer in small-scale local jobs. He is likely to parrot on about needing five 'O' levels, scaring the pants off local parents, not having heard that three-quarters of the school-leaving population have no likelihood of acquiring that score and manage without. He has little idea what the Certificate of Secondary Education (CSE) could tell him, nor much interest in the content of the examination curriculum. 'Can he spell? Will he do as he's told?' is all that one local employer wanted to know of a boy with no 'O' levels.

What is needed is more than a campaign to inform the public, parents and employers alike, of what is developing in schools today, though that is highly desirable. What is urgent is that both schools and employment should in some more co-ordinated and well informed way clarify their mutual expectations of each other. Employment should take a long look at what qualities it will need for survival into the twenty-first century and urge that such qualities should be fostered within the schools. A cool and reasoned calculation on these lines would, I suspect, show the need for totally different objectives from those designed to produce literate operatives a century ago and which still underlie much of the present unthinking demands.

In turn, teachers should stand up for a form of education in which equal value-rating is given to all students, despite their diverse aptitudes and interests, in which an individual is measured against his or her own potential, rather than against future earning power or some projected slot in the status-ranking of society. This view of education as 'normative' conflicts with the demands that it should be 'instrumental', serving to qualify students for some future use in society, or in further training. Schools almost inevitably incorporate elements of both the normative and the instrumental. We should betray our pupils if we did not prepare them to live in the world as it is, coming to terms with it in their several ways, to do their best in examinations and to find suitable openings in employment or institutions of higher education. Nevertheless, if we ever allowed the schools to become principally the sorting houses for the industrial society we at present live in, then we should be no better than the schoolmaster of the Latin story who led his pupils into the camp of their enemies. We cannot hope to give hostages against the future.

As a footnote on public expectation of schools and teachers, mention should be made of the increased attention being given to outbreaks of violence in schools. There is nothing particularly new about violence in schools, witness Thackeray's broken nose and the need for troops to be called in to quell riots at Eton and Harrow early in the last century. Violence has also been an essential feature in the teacher's control of his pupils with birch, tawse and cane. What is novel is that teachers have, by and large, sought to find a more civilised and civilising relationship with their pupils than one based on the rule of the stick, and they have often found that their relinquishing the stick has not necessarily been met immediately by a dropping of the fist. If a school that has used the stick is going to lay it aside, it must do so gradually, so changing attitudes on both sides that corporal punishment can be made to wither away. It will not wither away of its own accord, but for a headmaster to announce abruptly that as from today the cane will no longer be used, chaos is being invited. A new school, on the other hand, has a chance to start without ever using corporal punishment.

My own view is that in school violence breeds violence. If someone aimed a blow at my head I would try to pre-empt him with a quicker one, but then as time goes on one's reactions slow down and boys seem to get bigger. It is better to defuse situations that force showdowns. And the current anxiety over violence derives very largely from threats of confrontations in school.

Confrontations between adolescents, either in pairs or in gangs is largely a reflection of neighbourhood mores. After a schoolyard battle, nowadays as likely to involve girls as boys, in which someone is knifed or stabbed with a broken bottle, what can the teachers do other than send for police and ambulance, and send the others home to cool off?

This kind of violence, or more often the threat of it, is offered to the teachers mostly where they have allowed themselves to be conned by society into believing that they can form a front-line defence of law and order in a neighbourhood where law and order are being challenged. The teacher is a feeble substitute for a riot squad and it is astounding to realise how tolerant kids are of a teacher playing out that role when their numbers and size give them nothing really to fear from challenging his authority. If it comes to a showdown, the teacher cannot possibly win: he has to call in police patrols, as has happened already in American city schools. It is only when the school as an institution is itself threatening violence to its students that teachers need go in more fear of suffering attack than citizens in other walks of life locally.

I have visited many inner-London schools over the last few years, several of them as a regular caller, a student-supervisor, for whom nothing is staged and from whom little is hidden. With regard to violence, it was most remarkable that schools of comparable circumstances—in buildings, social background, percentage of immigrants, size, and so on—should differ so markedly in the degree to which their attendant atmospheres spoke of impending violence, or the lack of it. In one you could all but touch the air of battle, with either side observing a slender truce line, the teachers tensed to maintain their uneasy command. In another, teachers and kids alike, were relaxed, able to communicate without the strain of keeping a guard up, and as a result teaching and learning more. There was no less noise or movement: just that one was pleasant to be in and the other disturbing. I attributed the difference to the two contrasted collective attitudes of the teaching staffs in the two types of school. In the first they were concerned to hold down students in the fear of losing control over them, with the result that their control was constantly threatened. In the second, the teachers had individualised relationships far more, a high degree of trust had grown up between teachers and students with the result that situations were more likely to be negotiated than to be fought out.

In the first school, teachers felt that they were sitting on a time bomb and, as a result, they were. As long as the inner-city school preoccupies itself with enforced attendance, standardised styles of work, dress, behaviour and imposed goals, so will its unwilling students, drawn increasingly from socially deprived homes, in due course turn on that school as the nearest and clearest target for violent reaction to what society is forcing them to accept. The teachers cannot win by ever-more efficient repression, and they should, for the sake of their own skins if not for the human dignity of their students, resist the demands of society's spokesmen for law and order that they should hold the schoolkids down. Riots are usually sparked off by the over-reaction of frightened men.

If there is a time bomb of violence under our society then it is not going to be defused by resolute teachers, as some people imply. At the same time, though, there is no reason why teachers should offer themselves to the adolescent as the embodiment of social repression. If they do, they are going to need more protection than they will get. The teacher's first responsibility is to his students and if, as in my second type of school, he knows those students and is seen to be committed to their needs, he will gain their respect rather than risk their violence. It is those who cry to us for ever more increasing 'discipline' who will find the bomb go off in their faces.

## CHAPTER SIX

# Training and Prospects

There are two standard routes into teaching. One is by way of university and the other through a College of Education. The university route entails three years' study for a first degree. This does not necessarily carry any education content, in the sense of being related to the *teaching* of the subject studied, but it is followed by a one-year course at a university education department, leading to certification. A course at College of Education takes three years, resulting in qualification, with the opportunity for some students to study there for four years to obtain teaching qualification and the BEd degree. The result of this dual routing is a division amongst teachers that can be bitter and longlasting. Although it has now become obligatory for new entrants to teaching to have trained and qualified, either at College of Education or post-graduate university department, a large number of head teachers are still untrained graduates and the notion of necessary professional training still needs time to take hold.

The division is explained in part by history. The old foundation schools were headed for the most part by men in holy orders and staffed by university men. Before the great educational watershed of 1870 when Forster's Education Act introduced compulsory popular education, the majority of schools were church schools and the training of teachers was carried out almost entirely at residential colleges maintained by the various religious denominations. The expansion of the school population during the last quarter of the century saw a corresponding growth in the number of denominational training colleges.

The state had for long assisted church colleges with public money in exchange for standards that satisfied Her Majesty's Inspectors, and until the turn of the century depended heavily on the Church for an adequate supply of teachers. However, secular training entered the field, first with the appearance from 1890 onwards, of day training colleges attached to universities, and from 1904 with the establishment of teacher training colleges by the newly formed local education authorities. (Mr Balfour's Education Act of 1902 replaced the 2,568 School Boards by 328 local education authorities.) It was not until the 1950s, with the post-war impetus of R. A. Butler's 1944 Act, that the local education authority colleges outnumbered the denominational ones. At present there are some 170 Colleges of Education training teachers, of which some fifty are still denominational.

Mr Balfour's Act of 1902 established not only local education authorities, which in turn built training colleges, but also more grammar schools to augment the old foundation schools in providing secondary education for the selected minority. Pupils attending either paid fees or entered on scholarship from their elementary school. It is interesting to note as one of the recurrent evidences from history of man's unpredictable aspirations, that the creation of free places at the grammar schools produced a flood of applicants, far more of whom were capable of secondary education than could find places, turning what was intended as a special provision into the intense competition that became known as Eleven Plus. The competitiveness made places all the more coveted and for elementary school teachers it elevated the status of the grammar school into that of a Valhalla. The gods of this pantheon however were of a different birth.

The teachers in the grammar schools were recruited very largely from the universities, entering teaching immediately upon graduation. In 1911 it became necessary to hold a degree before entering a university department of education. By the following year there were nine universities with such departments: Birmingham, Durham, Leeds, Liverpool, London, Manchester, Oxford, Reading and Aberystwyth, with the number growing. But in spite of this, their students were few in number. Between 1908 and 1921 a total of no more than 2,761 students followed postgraduate training for teaching, and of those only 582 were men, an average of fewer than 45 a year. This admittedly covers the war years, but even allowing for that, it indicates a widespread disregard for the need to train. Although since that time the number of graduates training before starting to teach has risen steadily, to the point where a degree on its own no longer qualifies a teacher, there remains a lingering myth, fostered especially by older graduates in the schools, that a teacher is born and not made, that you either have it or you haven't.

I have never understood quite why this should be said of teachers and not solicitors or chartered accountants, except in so far as certain basic characteristics, such as patience, sense of humour, liking for children, are necessary prerequisites. These may have been enough to equip a gentleman down from Oxford to undertake the tutoring of a gentleman on his way up to Oxford, and it may well have been this nostalgic ideal that has trickled its way on through the consciousness of teachers in grammar and independent schools, but if that is all you have up your sleeve you won't be much use to a class of juniors with mixed reading disabilities needing to be diagnosed and remedied, nor will you last five minutes when shut in a classroom with thirty unmotivated adolescents. One major contributory reason for the myth has been the academic tradition that exalts the teacher's specialist knowledge. Within this tradition, if the pupil is exposed to 'a first class mind', usually taken to mean someone with a first class degree, however long ago it was acquired, and however garrulous its holder may have become, it is supposed that this quality of mind will rub off on to the pupil. The tradition hardly takes account of the *relevance* of the specialist knowledge to the total curriculum or to changing circumstances. The first class degree gives no guarantee, unfortunately, that its bearer will ask of what use it will be to his pupils a generation, or two generations later.

Some of the scorn directed by grammar school graduate teachers towards the notion of training arises from a belief that it consists mostly of techniques given to the novice by college lecturers who are failed university teachers who would be unable to teach a class in school if they ever tried. It is of course useful to learn techniques before trying to employ them, even how to write on a blackboard or use an overhead projector, but these can be acquired while on the job in school. What the period of training must offer above all during the period before the plunge into the hurly-burly, is the confrontation of the student with ideas about the purpose of education and a demand for him to work out a supportable theoretical justification for what he is setting out to do. All too soon he will be clutching desperately at whatever is expedient because it will work, pressed to take his lead from an examination syllabus, or seduced by the attractive packaging of the latest set of fashionable materials. If he has not at least the basis for a rationale of teaching, develop it and adapt it as he may in the light of study and debate, he will end up with nothing but the unsubstantiated and unshakable opinions that so often characterise the untrained teacher.

The entry qualification by the time of World War II was in general the holding of a 'School Certificate'. Some had passed through sixth form to obtain the Higher School Certificate. Since the war, the entry standards have risen steadily. The minimum requirement is five passes at 'O' level of the General Certificate of Education, but by 1967 there were 63 per cent of entrants who had passed one or more 'A' level subjects and fewer than 10 per cent with the bare minimum of five 'O' levels. It is of interest to note that at that date some 37 per cent of entrants held the usual minimum requirements of two 'A' level passes for university entrance. However, university entrance figures also reflect the steady increase in standards so that 73 per cent of undergraduates at university had three or more passes at 'A' level, with at least one of these at grade A or B, while only 9 per cent of entrants to Colleges of Education had such qualifications. There is every reason to think that many who enter Colleges of Education do so as a second best to entering university as much as out of any strong desire to teach. Not that this means they are any less likely to become good teachers eventually.

A sixth-form student wanting to teach would be well advised to find a copy of the Compendium of Teacher Training Courses in England and Wales. It is issued free by the Department of Education and Science to all schools. The student may decide to apply for university, either because of good 'A' level prospects or because, further to that, they are not sure that they want to teach, but if the route is to be by college, then there will be numerous prospectuses to look through. After applications come interviews. Colleges vary widely in methods of interviewing, from those where quarter of an hour with the principal is thought to be enough, to others where the applicant is seen by a succession of staff interviewers who carefully collate their impressions.

There is a long tradition of provision for training of mature students, but the proportion has increased steadily over the last two decades. One of the headaches of the DES has been the high rate of dropout from teaching by young women who train, expensively, for three years and then after the same period in school resign to have a baby. Most of those I have known swear on leaving that they will be back within two or three years, but they usually have underestimated the preoccupation that their first baby will cause and the speed with which teaching will drop astern. However, since the ministry of Sir David Eccles in the fifties, a steadier flow of trained women returning to teaching has been maintained (known ungraciously in the trade as m.w.r.—married women returners). These women bring a great breath of life into school, organising their work within strict hours, but the saner for having the counterbalance of husbands with totally different workaday concerns. Increasingly these women are taking on teaching responsibilities while their children are in infant schools, not waiting as formerly until they have left school. As a result, and it is one of the most significant changes in staffing over the last twenty years, the married women returners are returning while still au fait with developments and taking over responsibilities that open up careers, instead of coming back when it is too late to enter the promotion stakes. In terms of power, the married women have replaced that almost extinct breed of dedicated spinsters who used to occupy the positions of headmistresses and senior mistresses.

In the normal way, a student following the three-year course at a College of Education will find three strands in the curriculum. The first will be the 'main course', made up from a broad range of recognisable subjects, including English, Mathematics, History and so on. In some colleges the student need follow only one main subject, but usually there is a requirement to combine at least one other, either in parallel or as a subsidiary subject. A main subject will be followed to a level equivalent, generally speaking, to that of university pass degree. Although the main subject is a continuation of the student's personal education, it is obviously going to provide a main teaching subject, so that its content is related to the needs of subject teaching in school. For that reason, if for no other, some colleges now introduce inter-disciplinary main courses, such as combined Humanities.

The second strand in the college courses is contributed by 'curriculum studies'. This is the main professional element, introducing the student to the range and balance of subjects taught in the school and the theoretical ground upon which they are based. Those intending to teach in primary schools stand in particular need of a knowledge of the range of subjects beyond their special main course, but the timetable can become cluttered for the student to a point where only a superficial knowledge of these subjects may result. It is easy for the student to suffer from the same sense of fragmentation experienced by a secondary school student before the level of sixth-form specialisation.

The college curriculum represented by these two strands is heavily subject-centred, and on their own would only reinforce the nineteenth-century tradition of feeding children to a prescription of particular subjects, basically as Mr M'Choakumchild learnt to do. The essential third element, introduced to tip the balance towards a child-centred conception of teaching, is the Education Course. This itself combines features usually set in tension amongst each other for the student. There will be a study of History of Education, a study of Methods, and a study of Educational Psychology and Sociology. The trend over the past decade or two has been towards a more co-ordinated study of child development arising from this last element. 'Method' is seen increasingly as a function of the subject taught and pupil-teacher relationships, rather than a register of techniques that can be learnt in abstract for later application to whatever classes are being taught in school, rather as First Aid can be learnt in readiness for the unexpected discovery of anonymous sufferers.

The level of attainment by college students has risen in keeping with the increased academic standing of college staff and it is now possible to expect of students that they study the theoretical backing of what would otherwise be mere hunch or school folklore concerning the forces at play in a child's development and learning. William Taylor, Director of the University of London Institute of Education, has put this forcefully this way:

> The relationship of 'Education' to its underlying disciplines is in the same order as the relationship of the practice of medicine to the study of anatomy, physiology, biology and so on. Whether he is conscious of the fact or not, the medical practitioner is making use of such biological and physiological knowledge at every step of his diagnosis and recommendations for treatment; the teacher who denies the influence of social, psychological and philosophical assumptions in his own decision-making is merely the slave of unformulated and unsystematic patterns of habit.*

* W. Taylor, *Society and the Education of Teachers* (1969)

These three strands are woven into the whole college course so that they are interrelated. Colleges vary in the extent to which they attach importance to lectures. It is common practice to divide the course into units of half a term's length, each unit comprising lectures, leading to related seminars for small groups. Out of these arise the essays, or other assignments prepared by students individually and in groups. The units are in turn related to the other essential ingredient in the college course, school experience.

The teacher is never thrown in to the deep end of the nearest pool and left to sink or swim. There are many stages to pass through before the student first closes the door to shut herself into that classroom alone with thirty or so schoolchildren. Early in the course, students will visit schools, usually infants', to observe. This is just a taster. Observation is a skilled job, and early on the student will learn how to structure this observing so as to know what to look for and how to relate observations to what is already known.

The next stage involves getting to know some individual children. The students with small brothers or sisters, the aunts or uncles, have an immediate advantage: some students may well have had no contact with a small child ever, and may hold an image of the school pupil derived from his self-image as a sixth former, the last schoolboy he knew. Quite often the problem of finding something to say to a child, or discovering what will set them talking to you is the first obstacle the student has to overcome. I have myself as tutor to students in the stage of these early contacts often had one of them say 'But what do you think they might like to talk about?' I usually tell them 'Food'. That one always works.

Observation visits and the longer periods of practice are arranged by the college in schools within their area. There was a period, associated with the notion of Method as an abstract skill, when emphasis was placed upon 'model lessons' conducted by a Master of Method. For this purpose, many colleges had model classrooms to which borrowed school pupils (presumably model pupils) came for demonstration lessons and practice. In the United States colleges often have model schools on their campus still. But fortunately it is now recognised pretty universally that a model school is an unrealistic entity, by definition lacking just the dynamism and possibly the dynamite, that is the reality of school.

For older teachers the memory of 'demonstration lessons' dies hard. When I was a student in practice, the man to whom I was attached said apologetically one day, 'I suppose I should give you a demonstration lesson some time!' This struck me as odd since I had watched him teach on many occasions, but presumably he thought he ought to show me how it *should* be done rather than how he normally did it. Fortunately he forgot about it. But it was the college tutor who was supposed to show the student how it ought to be. It is a ludicrous supposition and one quite rightly abandoned in practice. I only once saw a college lecturer give a lesson in school to demonstrate to students. She did not know the class and the lesson was a disaster, for which she blamed the class as they misbehaved. (As well they might if they suspected they were being manipulated in such puppet play.)

The function of the college tutor is not to show the student teacher *how* it should be done, but to confront him with those issues and situations that will start him thinking about *why* it should be done, to teach him to observe others and to monitor his own work so that he can reflect on it and develop his practice. That and much more, but I see no reason why the college teacher should be expected to be able still to teach classes of school students as well as doing his own job. It might be a nice bonus if he can maintain some class teaching, but it is not a necessity, and with so much else to do, it would be a bit of a luxury. Of course, every schoolteacher, conscious of and jealous of the extra kudos carried by the title of 'lecturer', enjoys the occasional scoffing at those who supposedly presume to tell others how to do it, when, so the legend runs, they can no longer do it themselves, and probably only got out of schoolteaching because they were no good at it themselves anyway.

There are wide differences in the practical details of arrangements for college students during their school practice. Colleges cannot lay down regulations for the schools, only recommend. It all has to be agreed with utmost diplomacy on the college's part, each side guarding its prerogatives and often, as it was once put to me, 'cherishing their antagonisms'. Generally speaking though, a student is assigned to one mentor who will make introductions and iron out day-to-day problems. This mentor is best chosen from among the specialists with whom the student will be working principally. It may be the head of department or a reasonably experienced assistant. The mentor will negotiate a timetable of observation and teaching for the novice and initiate him into the routines of the teacher's life.

The practice period is to a great extent a process of induction, whereby the newcomer is allowed to feel what it is like to be 'of the staff', on duty and off. It is therefore of paramount importance that everything should be done to enable the student to see himself and to be seen as a young teacher, not as a learner. Learner he undoubtedly is, but then in a sense every teacher is. What is important though is that the student should be given every chance to find his feet as a teacher, not just be given classroom time to try out the techniques of imparting his subject. To this end, he should be taken into staffroom, given duties in harness with a form teacher, encouraged to join out-of-hours activities, invited to departmental and general staff meetings.

Although it is becoming more general, this kind of full induction is far from common. It is not as rare as it should be to hear of students not being allowed to use the staff common room, perhaps allocated some cubby-hole of their own, and it is still frequently heard that students should not under any circumstances attend staff meetings, on a variety of grounds, such as that confidential matters might be discussed. As if they were intruders rather than the new blood of our profession, standing to learn more about our concerns, attitudes and procedures from staff meetings than at any other time. Of course, they might start telling their grandmothers how to suck eggs, but if we couldn't survive that, then may the Lord help us.

The student's mentor is inevitably in an ambiguous position in that he is in part the guide, philosopher and friend, while being also in part the judge and assessor. The college will wish to let the practice period carry proper weight in the final assessment of the student's performance over the whole course, and yet it is virtually impossible to make fine comparative assessments of students one against the other in respect of their practice. Even in the same school, two students may be seen in quite different circumstances by a visiting supervisor from college, or even by one and the same mentor: they may teach classes with totally different collective characteristics, they will certainly vary in their own performance from day to day. What is the supervisor to ask of the mentor?

The supervisor may well visit the student only once or twice in the course of a month. He may have to travel miles daily to get round the schools where his students are in practice. He is bound to ask the school how things are going, and the mentor, having soon taken on something of a protector's role, possibly playing out the role of the groom-teacher wresting the bride-student from the mother-college, will tend to overpraise, or so to set the stage before the supervised lesson that it becomes something of a set-piece. The supervisor will need to tell both that a performance is not wanted, but rather a means of putting the observed lesson into a broader context by finding out what has led up to it and what is expected to develop from it. Above all the supervisor will look for growth points and give encouragement.

When I was tutoring students I used to tell them early in the course, 'You all think that because I have recently come here after many years of teaching, I must have learnt the trick of it and am going to reveal that trick to you. I assure you there is no trick and I am not going to tell you any secret for success. By the start of your first practice you will be hating me for not having told you how you are to do it. But, I repeat, I cannot tell you how to teach. Use me by all means as a flint on which to strike out your sparks or hammer out your basic attitudes, but from there you must work out your own solutions.'

Even so, at the time of the first visit as supervisor, I knew that the main question underlying all else the student might be saying, whether in tones apologetic or blustering, was, 'How am I doing, John?' And whatever else I had to say, above all I had to imply, 'You're doing fine.' Only rarely did I come across the student whose message was, 'I'm doing fine but the kids are unappreciative,' or 'The teachers here are a pack of fools who give me no help.' These were the impervious few who needed careful watching if they were not to develop into child-haters. These anxieties meant that the student expected a detailed criticism of a lesson observed by the supervisor, sometimes boldly demanded with some expression such as, 'Will you please be quite frank about where I may have gone wrong, as I am eager to learn.'

As supervisor you need to be quite firm. You do not know the class or how to deal with young Herbert in it who continually flips his neighbour's ear with his ruler. The school staff can answer that sort of thing with the fullness of experience. You can only help the student stand back from his own experience of the lesson and reflect on why he did this or did not do that. You can press him to speculate about alternatives; 'What would have happened if you had done this instead of that? You know the class, so would it have been better or worse that way, or a worthwhile risk?' You can suggest material that the student may not have considered, but he has to have the imagination to devise a use for it. Even the school mentor cannot say exactly what is the right way for the student to teach his class. The most important thing that all concerned can do, is to talk over and around the experience, so as 'to build up a kind of living composite map of the battlefield' (to borrow the phrase of Nicholas Otty in *Learner Teacher*).

All this means that the college has to mark on *its* map those schools where sympathetic guidance of students in practice is seen as a professional obligation rather than an inescapable necessity. Colleges will nurse their relationships with school, knowing how crucial to long-term attitudes will be their students' first responses. A number of colleges and university institutes have developed teacher-tutor schemes under which the school mentor is freed from school for some period, perhaps one day a week, to teach in the college, conducting a seminar, say, with a group that includes students due to practise in his school. He may be asked during his term of office to lecture on some aspects of his teaching, thus bringing closer the gap between theory and practice. This can lead to extremely valuable understanding developing between college supervisor and teacher-tutor.

The James Report to the government on the training of teachers in 1972 recommended a number of innovations. These included the recognition of the Colleges of Education as places of continued general education, extending secondary schooling in a manner comparable to, but not equivalent to university. The college could offer to its students a certificate of Higher Education and the option of continuing there to degree level if the intention was to teach. Another proposal was for the schools to take on a more precisely defined year of probationary training before the final year of post-graduate professional study. There is some merit in these proposals, cutting out as they do the time-wasting of college tutors trekking round a circuit of schools for isolated contacts, but they unfortunately suppose a level of expertise in training students on this scale in school that experience leads one to doubt may be found.

However, the James Report does lend weight to the notion that training cannot be a once-and-for-all matter. It has blurred the distinction between initial training and probation and it has also recommended sabbatical study leave of one term in every seven years of teaching. The committee was no doubt taking practical considerations into account, but my own recommendation would be for one full year every ten years. I would give the period of a whole year as it takes that long for anyone who is out of the habits of study to recover them. My experience of such in-service training is that it takes most of a term for teachers working together on a course to come out from behind their defensive positions and feel sufficiently reassured to look back on their old roles and appraise them objectively. And it certainly takes time for teachers to re-place their habitual reliance on opinion and experience with the evidences of true study and research.

If the Department of Education and Science could be persuaded of it, there would be no better place for it to put money than into expanding the in-service courses for experienced teachers. I have sometimes been heartbroken when interviewing selectively for such placings, looking for applicants to fill fifteen places funded by the DES when out of thirty interviewed all but the smallest handful of rather aimless shoppers-around would have warranted a place. These were men and women who had been in the fore-front of battle, often holding a school together over years of change and uncertainty, aware that ahead lay further change and uncertainty but that here at last was a year when the school might spare them to take a breather and ask themselves where they were going. I always tried to take those for whom the year chosen was crucial, possibly now or never, and those who genuinely seemed to sense that need for self-reappraisal.

The DES also promotes in-service courses in conjunction with the Area Training Organisations centred on the university Institutes of Education which are spread out over a period without breaking off teaching in the way that one-term or one-year courses do. These take various forms, but the basic pattern is one of an intensive session, say for a week, followed by one half day a week for six months, concluding with another intensive session. The content of the courses varies, offering aspects of educational theory and practice, but almost certainly a consideration of two particular current concerns.

The first major concern for senior staff on in-service training is curriculum theory and its application. This comes as a response to the awareness of how new and changing circumstances in society today call for new curricula to meet them and how these new demands call for revisions to staffing, resourcing and time-tabling. The other growing interest, or felt need, is in the methods of organisation in schools that will enable these new developments to function. Teachers are beginning to realise that much can be learnt about business efficiency from the field of management. By tradition we have looked askance at the world of commerce, priding ourselves on concern, by contrast, with human values, and too often thereby allowing the grossest incompetence to persist where a company secretary coming into school for a spell as a business consultant would have tidied up administration so as to make everyone's lives easier and more purposeful. There is danger that teachers, particularly head teachers or more especially aspiring head teachers, will become intoxicated with heady draughts of 'job analysis', 'decision networks' and the like, but the jargon can't do much harm and the insights gained can be invaluable.

Such training for senior staff has become inescapable in fact. For years after the war schools relied on staff in posts calling for administrative skills having learnt enough of this during experience in the forces. Many a subaltern who might have become an adjutant ended up as head of department or headmaster and any ex-sergeant would have a lot under his belt to help him as a housemaster. Now the teaching profession must produce its own managers. The trouble is that development of the teacher's skills, even though that nowadays involves a host of new organisational skills undreamt of by Mr Chips, does not in itself involve the skills of middle management required by senior staff in school over and above their teaching. The expertise in consultation, communication, forward planning, complex budgeting, group sociology and so on, is only going to come from outside and unless teachers train to understand and operate in these fields, they will find themselves increasingly managed by other professionals brought in by governors or local education authority.

I am not referring to the bursar or school administrator, who should be there anyway to handle money, standard returns, meals, caretakers, and such support services, but rather those who might replace the head or director of studies in order that the school may develop its structures of authority over the very matters of curriculum that lie at the heart of things.

One of the bugbears of teaching has been the way in which the basic salary has been related to initial qualifications, with little likelihood of much financial recognition of the increased competence that a teacher may develop with experience. Steady union pressure has done something to reduce the initial differentials between graduate and non-graduate, but little yet to give substantial reward to the teacher who just goes on becoming a finer teacher. To gain much increase in salary, the good teacher has frustratingly, to give up more and more teaching time, taking on other duties, planning, organising, becoming a head of department or a head teacher, or an adviser or an administrator. A full list of salary scales is shown in the Appendix, but one or two points may be noted about it here.

In the scales for 1972/3, the minimum starting rate for a three-year trained teacher was £1,179 rising on basic to £2,279. Most teachers can expect in time to add additional points to basic for responsibilities held. Some will rise to posts such as head of department which may carry up to four of these additional points which would bring a maximum salary of £3,277.

Another point to note is that there is equal pay between the sexes. The headmistress of a large school will command a salary of about £6,000 and will be among the very best paid women in the land.

Negotiating the salary structure is a cumbersome procedure. Any one round of negotiations seldom achieves more than adjustments here or there, but the politics involved make it hard to see clearly what it is that we are inching towards. By the time any policy has been achieved it is difficult to accept that it is not out of date in terms of the real needs. We have over a long period been approaching a basic salary on which it is possible for a married man to live. This is all well and good, but what now desperately needs to be built in to the structure is an incentive for the continuous in-service training that will be essential for maintaining the innovations of the 1960s and 70s. The demands upon a teacher's time and ingenuity and patience have risen, even where increased ancillary help has relieved him of some of his extra-professional tasks. The satisfaction of knowing that the added burdens of curriculum development are calls upon professionalism, rather than the mere donkey-work of such chores as dinner duties and supervision of bus queues, has a limited life. The teacher begins to feel like the Roman galley slave who is told that the emperor wants to go water-skiing and wonders when he will ever get paid for his extra pains. Sooner or later the teacher needs to have his time and competence reflected in his salary, otherwise we shall discover that the weary are falling back on to their basic salary for a short day and a short year, while the more energetic are evacuating from the classroom into administration, headship or teacher training.

# CHAPTER SEVEN

# New Roles for the Teacher

In 1847 Lord Macaulay in a speech to the House of Commons described teachers as:

> . . . the refuse of all other callings, discarded footmen, ruined pedlars, men who cannot work a sum in the rule of three, men who do not know whether the earth is a sphere or a cube, men who do not know whether Jerusalem is in Asia or America. And to such men, men to whom none of us would entrust the key of his cellar, we have entrusted the mind of the rising generation . . .

In response to this sort of concern there followed the period in which teachers were trained to accumulate a great ragbag of facts so that they could implant information, such as whether Jerusalem was in Asia or America, in the minds of the rising generation. At its worst it led to the useless pedantry of Mr M'Choakumchild; at its best to the mastery of subject disciplines with full academic respectability. But either way, the teacher could expect to be regarded as someone skilled in imparting his specialist knowledge, inducting his pupils into his own subject discipline. School provided an institutional framework that was upheld by society and backed the discipline required for that style of teaching and learning.

The schools were so organised that any one kind catered for the needs, or supposed needs, of one particular division of society:

a teacher knew, with a fair degree of accuracy, where his own pupils were meant to be going, and if any of them did not fit, he could recommend a transfer. A preparatory schoolboy was prepared for public school and a subsequent position of authority within society; a grammar school pupil was prepared for the middle class, taking and giving orders; an elementary schoolchild was going to make up the labour force. Once entry to grammar school was seen to provide a way out of the working class and therefore had become competitive, 'intelligence' was introduced as a discriminatory criterion, but this did not affect the way schooling was instituted for divided groups, except to harden the divisions. People were labelled by the kind of school they had attended. Edward Heath and Harold Wilson are still referred to significantly by some, as being 'grammar school men' rather than 'public school men'.

Just as the 1870 Education Act was introduced by W. E. Forster to provide industry with literate labourers, so the major changes introduced in the organisation of schools since 1944 have been motivated by society's need to have not just literate labourers but an educated population. The ideal of secondary education for all was a long time finding realisation, and long after the provision was made in terms of school buildings (however inadequate) and the retention of boys and girls in schools beyond the old elementary leaving age, the division of school pupils into hard groups has continued. Society has reflected in the attitudes of both government parties (allowing for flutters and fluctuations) its need to maximise and speed up the supply of innovative, skilled, adaptable and adventurous young people from the schools. The Newsom report to the government of 1963 reaffirmed that we were not yet tapping the sources within our rising generation that are needed to ensure national survival and prosperity. That is why it was entitled *Half Our Future*. The need to look to the whole of our future was the justification for accelerating the spread of comprehensive re-organisation and for the government circular 10/65 which required local authorities to draw up plans for reorganisation of their schools on comprehensive lines. What has not been sufficiently recognised, however, is that reorganisation and decree by central or local government will be of no avail in putting an end to divisive education unless the teachers have changed their attitudes fundamentally.

Up to now, their attitudes have changed only slowly. Teachers by origin have tended until lately to be conservative, and schools, like any hierarchical organisations, are internally resistant to change. So it was that the early comprehensive schools, the first purpose-built models of the late 1950s and the early 1960s, changed little inside them. The teachers had the authority to change the internal structures and methods, but lacked the confidence to do so. Within their glass walls they recreated the divisions then existing in the secondary system. 'Streaming' epitomises the whole system of divided education, deciding for children at their point of entry what is to be the provision for them within the school. The 'grammar school' children went into the top streams, the secondary modern, with their own gradings from 'borderline grammar' to 'remedial', into the rest. Teachers then regarded them in those lights and provided for them accordingly, and the prophecies implied in the divisions tended to be self-fulfilling. A perceptive but somewhat disillusioned young teacher once wrote to me:

When a kid in 3.3 said to me, 'But, Miss, I'm thick. We're all thick. We wouldn't *be* here if we weren't thick,' I said nothing because the truth would have sounded to him like an elaborate lie. This was my strongest reaction—that I was holding a ridiculously false position in a ridiculous system. The kids I felt happiest about were the ones who really caused trouble because they at least had some fight left in them. But these were the kids I was supposed to sit on, so that the rest could learn how to write formally humble letters beginning with Dear Sir and ending Yours sincerely, with a *small* s.

It is within this kind of reaction that can be found the strongest hope for a truly comprehensive education because this young teacher has seen the potential within her kids and at the same time the dehumanising, stunting effect upon a child of telling him through the institution itself, with no one needing to state it in words, that he must be thick. If teachers had actually said 'You are the thickies', or 'This is the dimmies' class', the kids might have resisted the suggestion, but if they learn it by the very way the country and its teachers have established their school system, then either it *is* true, or the system is ridiculous. Unless, that is, someone has a vested interest in making sure that most of our children *are* conned into becoming thickies. Though there were those in power at the start of the Victorian era anxious to keep the nation that way, no one looking after even their own interests could wish it to remain like it today. Or could they?

When teachers have realised what Newsom was proclaiming urgently a decade ago, that the majority of our children are achieving nothing like their own potential best, and, what Newsom failed to perceive, that the system of divided provision is a major contributory factor in the failure, shall we find an adequate change of approach among teachers. That change is coming about, but it is painful, and as with all change, it makes demands upon teachers that produce strains, with all too often insufficient public support for the new roles that they are called upon to play.

The new roles are called for by a curriculum and organisation that will create schools open to all comers, rather than just certain sections of the child population. Our primary schools have been meeting this challenge for over two decades and are still wrestling with the inherent problems. Comprehensive secondary schooling is relieving them of the main cause of division in their upper years, selection at Eleven Plus for a separative second stage, but the battle to achieve acceptable standards, in literacy for instance, is still on. In the reorganised comprehensive system, the tasks required of the teachers are only beginning to be recognised. What are they?

The essence of the new schooling is that it accepts the given, the pupils of its district, rather than some section or other carved out from it. And it accepts them not as all being alike, or even forming a number of identifiable groupings, but as differentiated individuals, all different, but equally valued as such. That is what comprehensive schooling is about, not some convenient new form of organisation. Its analogy is the family. To the parents of a caring home, all the children are of equal value, but their differing characteristics, stages of development, interests and passions, whether passing or abiding, call for varied attention and deployment of resources. There is only uniformity of care. If one is ill, he receives extra attention; if one is going abroad, she may warrant extra expenditure; each learns to take turns, share out, give and take, as long as mother and father are just and fair. If one does well in some venture or other, whether swimming a mile, saving his earnings to buy a guitar, winning an egg and spoon race or passing five 'O' levels, he is given praise, but not at the expense of humiliating the brothers and sisters. Each is supported and encouraged, so that security and confidence enable them to stand on their own feet and in due course step out unafraid into the world, knowing the meaning of justice and trust and loyalty, but strong to face the injustice, deceit and treachery of the world and the cut and thrust of competition. In the family we can only approximate to that ideal, but caring parents are committed to striving after it, abandoning the desire to dominate, releasing its members into the fullness of determining their own destinies. And the same must hold true of the common school, wanting no less than equal justice for all the children in its care and granting them eventual autonomy.

For the teacher, this carries a number of implications. As I mentioned in the chapter on training, the teacher can no longer regard himself as primarily a subject specialist. A secondary teacher is almost bound to specialise and should have a close understanding of the nature of at least one discipline of learning, but, as his primary school colleagues have for long seen, the specialism is subordinate to the call to regard his pupils as individuals, each with the need for an integrated curriculum that is seen on all sides to make sense. It is nothing new for the good teacher to care for the well-being of his pupils or to know them as individuals, but in secondary schools, grammar and modern, this has for the most part been carried out only within the selective framework that separated 'academic' from 'pastoral' guidance, and grouped pupils together on curriculum decisions made by someone else. Now he needs to provide curriculum guidance for all kinds of pupils committed to him.

In a prophetic article* Dr Eric Midwinter writes about the urgent need for relevance which our specialist system is failing to provide. 'By weaving a weft of subject threads across the warp of class strands (and sometimes adding a third thread of the "house" system), an overtight and stifling mesh is completed which is unable to cope with the needs of particular children faced with particular problems in particular areas.' His own offered solution is one being developed already at Countesthorpe, teams of mixed specialists leading groups of students in longer-term examinations of realistic issues. 'Combined studies' of this sort are no longer new, but have seldom yet taken the central position in curriculum for all, only for primary age levels or in secondary school for the so-called 'less academic'.

Now teaching like that means that the specialists in the mixed teams need to find a totally different starting point from the traditional one of asking, 'What in my specialist knowledge should I select as appropriate to this given group of pupils, and how should I teach it?' Instead he needs to ask, 'What concerns these particular students, whether it is football, local political issues or violence? Are they grouped according to common interests? How can my specialist knowledge contribute to any study in depth of these concerns and interests? How will my contribution balance with the provision made by other specialists?'

Such a way of approaching teaching makes three distinct kinds of demand on the teacher, who will then in turn have certain demands to make of the system within which he is working. The

* 'Alienation by Sixteen', *Forum* vol 15, no 2, Spring 1973

first is that in order to know what his students are really concerned about, or could become concerned about, rather than to speculate as to what they *might* be concerned about, he has to get to know them by being involved with them. The good teacher has always known a lot more about his pupils than how many marks they have been getting in his subject, but the subject has traditionally been something existing apart from the pupil, to be studied, but not particularly related to immediate needs. The new demand is for the teacher to know his pupil so well personally that he can discover from within the learner what the subject has to offer. This requires a relationship of much greater familiarity, involving as it does mutual trust. Previously it didn't much matter if the pupil and teacher liked each other. It helped, but it wasn't essential. What was needed was a syllabus, motivated pupils and a teacher trusted over interpretation and organisation. Now the teacher has to get very much closer, be prepared for the reactions and knocks that often accompany personal involvement, make a lot of time available for talking, accept colloquial familiarity, and generally to take the emotional strains involved. He will need to know the homes of his students and will therefore undertake home visiting, adding parents' strains to those of their children. Parents usually welcome this giving of time to understanding their children better, but they may well raise an eyebrow at the easing of formalities which enabled teachers previously to preserve a social distance, but which would now possibly prevent the contact sought for. All this is time-consuming and tiring.

The knowledge that the teacher gains from such social proximity to his students needs to be pooled with that gained by his colleagues about theirs, so that it can be related to their teaching programme. And here the teacher will find another set of novel demands. Hitherto, however much the teacher had to conform to the general rituals and arrangements in a school, and though he had no hand in deciding the selection of pupils assigned to him, in his own classroom he reigned supreme. Provided his work did not disrupt others, and he obtained satisfactory results, he was autonomous, styling his teaching as he wished. It was probably fairly uniform, but there was always room for eccentrics. The trend now is towards greater freedom over curriculum and syllabus, but with teachers trading increased co-operation and team work for a reduction in individual autonomy. If you plan group teaching in any way, then what you wish to do as teacher is limited by what the others grouped with you will accept. So you have to get to know and understand not only your students, but also your fellow teachers, and learn to get on with them.

If this is not a steep enough order, consider also that the teacher will be stepping outside the security of a safely familiar subject into the uncertainties of a demand from his students for guidance through unpredictable areas of learning. It is not that the specialist has to descend to being a general teacher, a jack of all trades and master of none. That would be to overlook the change of approach, to suppose that the teacher is imparting knowledge in the same manner but over a wider field. What the teacher will be doing increasingly is helping his students to identify their problems but then, instead of giving the solutions, directing them to the means of solving them. This entails the teacher becoming expert in locating the sources of knowledge, identifying the techniques of problem-solving and either teaching these techniques or putting the student in touch with those specialists who will do so. He has to set up situations that will pose problems in such a way and at such a time that his students, whose motivation he will have studied, will want to solve them. The problems may range from how to trace a family history in local archives to how to establish a telephone exchange system. Above all, the teacher will need to be skilled in shaping purposeful discussion so that instead of going round in circles it may crystallise issues without his providing answers or imposing his opinions. To do this he has to lead without dominating and to introduce material, either to provide evidence or to pose questions. Since the material may be printed, may be visual or may mean introducing a human witness, whether a fellow teacher, a local vicar, doctor or tradesman, the teacher needs to learn what he can make available. In a word he has to be resourceful.

But, to repeat the comment of Chapter 3, he cannot be content with being simply an agent. He also has to initiate, to challenge and to make demands, physical and intellectual on each and all of his students. In saying that he has to restrain himself from imposing his opinions, it is inescapable that he will champion certain values if he is to remain worthy of the name of teacher rather than technician. He will champion the involvement of emotion rather than its suppression, but see it given shape, and balanced by reason. He cannot but stand for rationality as opposed to irrationality, even if he always takes account of the irrational. He needs to ensure that both Apollo *and* Dionysus are paid their proper dues. He will also encourage persistence and the value of deferred satisfaction in order that a job can be seen through to completion.

This latter value has of course been the justification by teachers in the past of introducing work which has seemed pointless to pupils at the time, boring and alienating all those who were not already prepared to accept long-term goals. To do this is to lose all those pupils who are accustomed to more immediate satisfaction, so the teacher has to win this point step by step, perhaps over years, so that its value is gradually learnt, not assumed to be there or else permanently lacking in a pupil's character. He will need to start from the more immediate satisfaction, particularly that of seeing that the work in hand has recognisable relevance to the student. To quote Eric Midwinter again:

> The five years of secondary life is a long and important time in anyone's life. We should not spend all of it looking to the future and preparing youngsters sternly for that future. They are alive now. They should be given the joy and satisfaction of exciting and inspiring experiences, because they are human beings who, here and now, deserve such treatment.

If the teacher is to accept all comers and value them all equally, with all their differences, in ability, social class, manners and appearance, he has also to be acceptable to them. Yet with such diversity he cannot be all things to all men. He must be himself, but he must also tolerate diversity among his colleagues. For too long the teacher has been required to present an image of middle-class respectability. There is a danger that in working with all conditions of students, he may be seen to identify the educational values of mutual care, rational thinking, persistence and deferred goals, with middle-class values of a purely superficial kind, like white collars and posh accents. If this happens, then for a large proportion of school students, the package deal is off. It is horrific to consider how many school leavers leave behind them the possibilities of planned enjoyment or reasoned argument because they were seen as invariably accompanied by twin-set and pearls or grey suit and waistcoat. This is not to argue that teachers should cultivate bother boots and a glottal stop, but it does suggest that if these are a teacher's preference then they should be accepted both by training college and by school, unashamedly and unself-consciously.

This is only one aspect of the way in which teachers will increasingly be asserting themselves. There are others of greater significance. Two pointers lead to this conclusion. The first arises from the more demanding nature of the work itself. The teacher who is expected to bring up his students to solve problems by making decisions affecting their own development will expect to exercise parallel prerogatives himself. Moreover, if he is released from the private domain of his classroom and required to deploy organisational skills over a wide number of matters involving resource material, their costing, the work programmes of ancil-laries, the increased contacts of the outside world, then he is going to expect a vastly increased say in the policy-making of the school as a whole. The teachers, instead of retiring to work in their independent cells, are becoming increasingly affected by each others' decisions and will therefore want joint control of the situation. The alternative would be more and more people telling him what to do, which would rapidly become intolerable.

The other pointer is the increased demand for self-determination among students. It is hardly surprising if we increasingly encourage students to think for themselves and take responsibility for their own actions, that they should become teachers who will no longer be content to carry out instructions without question. We have taught them to question and should not be surprised to find them increasingly radical. In an older, more stable order, it was possible for a school to treat its young members of staff as if they were embarking on a long novitiate at a monastery. If an institution is governed by traditions and precedent, interpreted by those versed in the lore (and schools had their priest/lawyers just as Mervyn Peake's *Gormenghast* had its Sourdust), then it was right and proper for the novice to sit quiet and listen until after the appropriate rite de passage. In a time of change, as has always been discovered by a general staff in time of war, when innovation is at a premium, it is not the old men who come up with the saving ideas, but the young men with the sharpness of fresh minds. Older teachers, just like older managers or generals, will try to select circumstances that fit their methods and ignore what is left uncovered, or blame it for being awkward, rather than face altered circumstances and adapt their practice to meet them. That is why awkward questions in the staffroom are not welcome. However, when a newcomer in school now asks, 'Why do you do it this way?' it will no longer do, as it may have done once, for the establishment to reply, 'Because that is the way we have always done it,' implying, 'And the sooner you learn that, young fellow, the better.'

There has always been the danger of teaching attracting its recruits from amongst those most anxious to find security. The new danger is that the urgent need for change in schools will cause that change to come from outside pressure and initiative if it is not forthcoming internally. Therefore we need to attract innovative and adventurous entrants, and to hold them. Some of the ablest and most original young graduates I now meet who are trained to teach, drop out after their first spell of teaching or practice, not for the more obvious deterrent reasons such as the personal threat of the classroom, lack of sympathy with the young and adolescent, but for a reason that I find much more disturbing. I am referring to students who have chosen to teach, not as a last resort and certainly not as an academic refuge, an alternative to research or writing a novel. These are the men and women who want to teach because they see that children need a new provision: they are the ones who have discerned, with or without Alvin Toffler, that, as he puts it in *Future Shock*, 'we shall need first to generate successive, alternative images of the future' and that 'it is only by generating such assumptions, defining, debating, systematizing and continually updating them, that we can deduce the nature of the cognitive and affective skills that the people of tomorrow will need to survive the accelerative thrust.' They are the adventurous but altruistic young whose contemporaries going into industry, marketing, publishing and elsewhere in the competitive world will be expected to make a mark within two years, be given the scope to do so, and know that if they fail, they will be out of a job. Coming into school, prepared to make an equal commitment of time and ingenuity, they find instead that far from being invited to contribute 'alternative images of the future' they are being expected to keep quiet and learn their business for the first two years. And many find that life is too urgent after four years training to wait longer for things to happen.

Now there is everything to be said for learning your business, and it will take all of two years in school for a young teacher to do so, but it won't take a bright beginner even two months to discern where the power lies in an organisation, where some fresh ideas could be helpful and what sort of response the organisation makes to new ideas. Let the probationer learn tact and some humility, let him learn from the experience of the past, since many things about schools will still repeat themselves. But at the same time, schools must devise organisational structures, and the older men and women must adopt accompanying attitudes, that will allow for innovatory drive to spring from any source. And this, as the average age of those in full-time education continues to rise, will increasingly include the school students.

In fact, if schools close their ranks to these awkward young teachers, who really intend to help 'the people of tomorrow . . . to survive the accelerative thrust', although some of them will move into other occupations, many of them will side-step the system to work in alternative forms of education. There has been since the start of the 1970s a growing debate over the issue of whether schools can survive as institutions at all. The cry has gone up, often with ill-thought-out sensationalism, 'School is dead'. De-schooling has not only been proposed as a worked-out method of providing for the learning that children need, but has been put into effect at Free Schools and Shopfront Schools, first in the United States and Scandinavia, and now in England. In areas where school-refusal is high ('truancy' suggests a more occasional absence and hardly fits the long-term avoidance covered by this term), and clearly linked to the social problems of housing, poverty and health, young teachers have set up centres for drop-out children to drop-in.

The whole atmosphere of these 'schools' is very different from anything either the kids or the teachers are likely to have experienced within the system. For a start, the premises are likely to be buildings that no one else wants, a disused warehouse or condemned housing that the teachers patch up themselves. There would be no rules that had not been agreed between teachers and children, no fixed hours or curriculum, only a place to use, and teachers willing to teach what anyone expressed a need to know. So far the 'free school' movement has managed on shoe-string finance, wringing at most a recognition out of local authorities, who, it must be faced, are tight pressed over money to administer their own services to Educational Priority Areas. Some of their money problems derive from their teachers' own scorn for institutions and open hostility to the maintained system, which is high-handed since they themselves need to institutionalise to become more than a casual and ineffective gesture towards the problem.

The experience in Scandinavia has been different and certainly more methodical. There the initiative over free schools came from students, not teachers. In Oslo for instance, drop-outs from the formal gymnasiums, of ages 16 to 18, formed their own school, hired their own teachers, elected one as *skolleder* (head teacher), and then organised a political campaign for regular government finance in terms that no party could decently oppose. The Forsøksgymnaset is thus an autonomous, publicly financed institution, governed jointly by its students and its teachers. Such a development would be possible here though there are no signs at present of such an initiative. In any case, neither our own 'free schools' nor those abroad are going to remedy situations that arise from social conditions totally unrelated to schooling—poverty, monotony, overcrowding, and crime. What we are left with is the challenge summed up in Paul Goodman's comment: 'I doubt that, at present or with any reforms that are conceivable under present school administration, going to school is the best use for the time of life of the majority of youth.'*

There is not space here to discuss the various possible alternatives to an extended compulsory education, any of which could turn out to be just more of the same. My own choice for reasonable success is the 'open-access' school which will erase the boundary lines between schooling, recreation, and adult education. It will be the centre for full-time and part-time non-vocational courses for those approaching and beyond the age of compulsory attendance. It should be parallel to, but not imitating the vocational College of Further Education. It will prepare students for public examinations at 16 and 18, but it will not hinge its work unduly on their syllabuses. It will provide for fun activities, ranging from boat-building to drama, it will be open to the local public and it will tap the resources of that public in return, using them for the benefit of its students.

More and more local authorities putting millions of capital into the plant of large senior schools want to see a greater use

* *Compulsory Miseducation* (1962)

made of them by the public whose money has gone into them. It is lunacy to leave them idle for the greater number of waking hours in the day. So the school will also house the public library, infant welfare clinic, and old people's club room. I have already seen situations where the atmosphere makes it easy for a young mother to leave her children in crèche while joining fifth and sixth formers for 'O' and 'A' studies. It will not be strange much longer to find mother and daughter in the same 'sixth form'. At present such mature students pay FE rates for their classes, but it would not be difficult to introduce some system of educational vouchers enabling all school leavers to claim x number of years free education at a time and place of their own choosing. Perhaps instead of compulsory school from 15 to 16, many would prefer it ten years later. The experience of the Swedish Folk High Schools has shown that the demand for late courses for adults is never-ending.

All this in turn makes more demand on the teacher. He will no longer be so sure of whether he is a secondary teacher or an FE teacher. Certainly he needs to know where to cry halt before he becomes a welfare worker. But all this should be accommodated if we are to accept change as part of the way of life. The teachers' unions will themselves be re-examining the nature of their memberships. At present their very multiplicity speaks of hardened specialisms, and they may well act as a brake on the development of the new roles for teachers because of their tendency to defend the status quo. Mobility of function among members will only be maximally easy when there is one union for all teachers, as there is for instance in Canada. In the meantime we spend too much of our effort warring between ourselves.

There are at present ten organisations for schoolteachers and FE college staff alone. The division, and the consequent differentiation of attitudes towards the status of teachers, leaves open the final question of whether teachers can regard themselves as in any sense a profession at all. Their main body, the NUT, certainly regard themselves as a trade union. Who are the others?

Certainly the National Union of Teachers can claim the seniority of age and numbers. It was founded in 1870 and opens its membership to all teachers. Quite apart from retired members, the NUT claimed 188,500 serving teachers in 1971. It has a majority of women members, most of them serving in primary education. As a result, men teachers felt increasingly that the career needs of a married man were insufficiently represented in salary negotiation. The National Association of Schoolmasters formed as a breakaway from the NUT in 1922 but remained a very small body until women achieved equal pay in 1960. From that moment on its membership grew, doubled its size in twelve years and now claims over 50,000 men. It has maintained a militant attitude and carried out threats to strike on many occasions. One main effect of its noise has been to gain better representation on both the Burnham teachers' panel and on the Schools' Council.

A larger, more powerful if less vociferous body than the NAS is the Joint Four. It is an alliance of the Association of Assistant Mistresses, the Assistant Masters' Association, the Association of Headmistresses and the Headmasters' Association. Although there is nothing exclusive in their terms of membership, these four associations recruit mainly graduates and traditionally their strength derived from the grammar schools, though they now have considerable support from within comprehensive schools. Their total membership is about 56,000 serving teachers. One of the main grievances of the NAS is that with nearly as many members, they have half as many representatives on the Burnham teachers' panel. (NUT has 16 members, Joint Four has 6 and NAS only 3.)

Even the head teachers are divided. The Joint Four represents secondary school heads, with a very small sprinkling of primary school headmistresses, but most primary school heads belong to the National Association of Headteachers, which has about 14,000 serving members.

Far from there appearing to be any move towards a single representative body, the proliferation of new ones continues. In 1965 the Union of Women Teachers was formed with a hundred or two schoolmistresses who aligned themselves with the NAS as a militant body which by 1971 had attracted 14,000 members. In contrast, the Professional Association of Teachers was formed in 1970 with a vow never to strike, a call that rallied well over 4,000 members.

Neither UWT nor PAT has been granted representation on Burnham, but to complete the brief survey I should identify the ATTI, the Association of Teachers in Technical Institutions, which has about 35,000 members and a seat on the Burnham panel. There are several smaller specialist bodies such as the Association of Educational Psychologists and the British Association of Art Therapists, but most members of such minorities probably hold dual memberships or, as in the case of these two, affiliations to one of the larger groups.

From this may be seen the teachers' tendency to look for ideal solutions rather than a working compromise. Where the existing unions have fallen short of the highest principles, we have tended to form a new one that will be purer. Obviously this has led to weakening of any bargaining power and as a result many radical and militant young teachers have of late directed their energies into the NUT in the belief that strength can only be won by preserving the major union, but reforming it from within.

The other hope of teachers over the past century has been for the establishment of a professional council that would unite all teachers in a register of those qualified by criteria established by its members. They have looked to the self-regulation of the medical profession and tried to emulate it. (It is of course interesting to note that the General Medical Council was established in 1858 by the government, as a measure of protection for the public against quacks, and that a doctor has right of appeal against the GMC to the Privy Council.) Teachers have sought to have a similar body established by the government and are still trying after seventy years of successive failures.

The first Teachers' Registration Council was recognised in 1899. Its function was literally to maintain a register of qualified teachers. It fell into disrepute because from the start it established a dual standard of elementary and secondary lists. A renewed Council in 1912 had the support of the NUT and registered 40,000 teachers, which in turn led to the creation in 1929 of the Royal Society of Teachers. However, its hopes foundered on the fact that registration was never obligatory for teachers and nothing ever came of its promise of self-determination. The old divisions remained as strong as ever. It was not until 1964 that the unions again proposed a Teachers' General Council, and it was Edward Short, while Secretary of State for Education and Science, who set up a Working Party to look into the possibilities.

At the time of this publication it now seems unlikely that the proposals of that Working Party will gain the general support of the unions. One of the main demands of teachers seeking professional status has always been the control of qualification. The proposals published by the DES in 1970 ('A Teaching Council for England and Wales', Report of the Working Party) made it clear that the local education authorities, their colleges of education and the universities, were powerful enough to oppose a teacher council that sought to control the supply and training of teachers, and would undoubtedly do so. Given this central admission, none of the other details are of very much significance. The plain truth is that teachers are nowhere near achieving the professional status that is implied by a teachers' council having (a) a register, (b) control of qualification, (c) powers to discipline members, and (d) financial independence.

The movement towards a teaching council plods on, but events overtook it when in 1970 the NUT joined the TUC. Without going into the steps that led up to it, it is clearly the most significant expression by the teacher that the more restrained salary negotiations of the white-collar workers were leaving him behind in the face of the bargaining powers of the big unions. Although this move was accompanied by a demand from NUT rank and file membership for a 'closed shop', requiring all serving teachers to belong to a union, it is not yet sufficiently supported. In fact it is not clear what benefit will be gained by teachers from the TUC affiliation. Effective strike action by teachers had been carried out before 1970, and in future demands they will not find the TUC doing their work for them. It is probably a move that is above all psychological in that it aligns teachers, at least through their largest union, with the working class. Many claim that this is not incompatible with achieving professional status eventually, through an autonomous teaching council. But there is no denying that true to our tradition we stand divided.

In conclusion, though, I see no reason to be pessimistic over this situation. Teachers will have to fight together for just salaries and the country will correspondingly have to recognise the need to attract and hold those who can effectively prepare its next generation for challenges beyond the expectations of the school-teachers of yesterday. More than that, the country will need to find teachers who will maintain the continuous education of students of all ages, for we are already into the era where all of us need to go on learning for as long as we are active. The last two decades, with the successive raisings of the school-leaving age, the huge growth in higher education and the development of curricula in all fields, has seen a progressive blurring of the division between teaching and learning. No one has had to learn faster than the teacher and if his students are to be drawn increasingly from a larger and growing cross section of the whole population, then perhaps the most rewarding of the new roles that he may be expected to play will be that of lead-student among learners, more humble, more human, yet because of that, possibly more able to achieve respect and self-respect in an age of increasing uncertainties.

# Appendix

TEACHERS' SALARIES 1972-3

*Assistant Teachers*

| Scale | Minimum £ | Increments £ | Maximum £ |
|---|---|---|---|
| 1 | 1,179 | 78 (6), 83 (5), 108 (1) 109 after 3 years | 2,279 |
| 2 | 1,319 | 78 (3), 81 (1), 83 (8), 108 (1) | 2,406 |
| 3 | 1,591 | 94 (10) | 2,531 |
| 4 | 2,016 | 94 (10) | 2,956 |
| 5 | 2,429 | 106 (8) | 3,277 |

Where a teacher paid on scale 1 is entitled to be classed as a good honours graduate, the salary rates from the twelfth incremental point shall be:

| Incremental Point | 13 | 14 | 15 | 16 | 17 |
|---|---|---|---|---|---|
| Salary | £2,253 | £2,336 | £2,336 | £2,336 | £2,445 |

Where a teacher paid on scales 2 or 3 is entitled to be classed as a good honours graduate, the appropriate scale shall be extended by two increments of £83 per annum.

Assimilation of existing teachers to the recommended salary scales shall be by corresponding points.

The additions to be paid after 1 April 1972 to new entrants who are graduates will be £156, good honours graduates—£312, holders of merit allowances—£78.

The additional payment to teachers in schools of exceptional difficulty shall be £105.

The London Area payment shall remain at £118 until 31 October 1972.

Teachers who received a salary in excess of the maximum of their scale under the 1971 report will be safeguarded by a payment above the maximum of the 1972 Scale which is equal to the amount by which their salary exceeded the 1971 scale.

In schools in Group 10 or above, the local education authority shall have discretionary power to appoint up to three senior teachers. Each senior teacher shall count four points against the school's points score. The salary scale of senior teachers shall be £2,641 × £106 (8) – £3,489.

Schools in Group 3 (ie having a unit total or review average of 201–300) should have a points score range of 0–1, enabling one assistant teacher to be placed in Scale 2.

If a teacher, who has lost his post or whose salary would otherwise be diminished as a result of the reorganisation or closure of a school, continues as a full-time teacher in a primary or secondary school maintained by the same local education authority and is employed as such a teacher in a special school or class, he shall be entitled to receive both his safeguarded salary and the additional payment for teaching in a special school or class.

*Deputy Head Teachers*
Schools, other than special schools

| Group | Minimum £ | Increments £ | Maximum £ |
|---|---|---|---|
| 3 | 1,510 | 83 (10), 109 (1) | 2,449 |
| 4 | 1,772 | 94 (9) | 2,618 |
| 5 | 2,123 | 94 (7) | 2,781 |
| 6 | 2,655 | 94 (4) | 3,031 |
| 7 | 2,819 | 94 (4) | 3,195 |

| Group | Minimum | Increments | Maximum |
|-------|---------|------------|---------|
|       | £       | £          | £       |
| 8     | 2,971   | 94 (4)     | 3,347   |
| 9     | 3,178   | 94 (4)     | 3,554   |
| 10    | 3,353   | 94 (4)     | 3,729   |
| 11    | 3,500   | 94 (4)     | 3,876   |
| 12    | 3,658   | 94 (4)     | 4,034   |
| 13    | 3,794   | 94 (4)     | 4,170   |
| 14    | 3,947   | 94 (4)     | 4,323   |

Where a deputy head teacher is appointed to a school below Group 3, the scale applicable shall be: £1,456 × £83 (10) × £104 (1) – £2,390.

Special Schools

| Group | Minimum | Increments | Maximum |
|-------|---------|------------|---------|
| 3 (S) | 1,861   | 83 (9)     | 2,608   |
| 4 (S) | 2,094   | 94 (7)     | 2,752   |
| 5 (S) | 2,588   | 94 (4)     | 2,964   |
| 6 (S) | 2,795   | 94 (4)     | 3,171   |
| 7 (S) | 2,958   | 94 (4)     | 3,334   |
| 8 (S) | 3,122   | 94 (4)     | 3,498   |
| 9 (S) | 3,296   | 94 (4)     | 3,672   |

Where a deputy head teacher is appointed to a school below Group 3 (S) the scale applicable shall be: £1,628 × £83 (10) × £104 (1) – £2,562

*Head Teachers*
Schools, other than special schools

| Group | Minimum | Increments | Maximum |
|-------|---------|------------|---------|
|       | £       | £          | £       |
| 0, 1  | 2,213   | 83 (4)     | 2,545   |
| 2     | 2,343   | 83 (4)     | 2,675   |
| 3     | 2,485   | 83 (4)     | 2,817   |
| 4     | 2,655   | 94 (4)     | 3,031   |
| 5     | 2,895   | 94 (4)     | 3,271   |
| 6     | 3,189   | 94 (4)     | 3,565   |
| 7     | 3,484   | 94 (4)     | 3,860   |

| Group | Minimum £ | Increments £ | Maximum £ |
|---|---|---|---|
| 8 | 3,762 | 94 (4) | 4,138 |
| 9 | 4,072 | 94 (4) | 4,448 |
| 10 | 4,377 | 94 (4) | 4,753 |
| 11 | 4,683 | 94 (4) | 5,059 |
| 12 | 4,987 | 125 (3) | 5,362 |
| 13 | 5,292 | 125 (3) | 5,667 |
| 14 | 5,597 | 125 (3) | 5,972 |

Special Schools

| Group | Minimum £ | Increments £ | Maximum £ |
|---|---|---|---|
| 2 (S) | 2,527 | 83 (4) | 2,859 |
| 3 (S) | 2,696 | 83 (4) | 3,028 |
| 4 (S) | 2,866 | 94 (4) | 3,242 |
| 5 (S) | 3,138 | 94 (4) | 3,514 |
| 6 (S) | 3,422 | 94 (4) | 3,798 |
| 7 (S) | 3,721 | 94 (4) | 4,097 |
| 8 (S) | 3,939 | 94 (4) | 4,315 |
| 9 (S) | 4,140 | 98 (4) | 4,532 |

## POSTSCRIPT

(Written for a fourteen-year-old girl at Countesthorpe who asked me to say what I thought about my own school days at the end of a questionnaire she had devised.)

Thank you, Sharon.

Mine was a narrow, rigid education in isolated circumstances. We learnt to obey, not to question; to work hard under Spartan conditions. It was tough, but it was secure. Our masters were dedicated men and we all accepted the arrangement. It made us into excellent soldiers, but pretty inadequate civilians. Most of my life, all of it since twenty-two, has been civilian. It is better to learn how to live to be a civilian.

# Bibliography

Bernstein, B. 'Open Schools, Open Society?' *New Society* (26.2.70)

Bourne, Richard. 'Who Are the Teachers?' (NUT, London, 1969)

Castle, E. B. *A Parents' Guide to Education* (Penguin, 1968)

Clegg, A. B. *Delinquency and Discipline* (Councils and Education Press, 1962)

Douglas, J. W. B. *The Home and the School* (MacGibbon and Kee, 1964)

Hannam, C., Smyth, P. and Stevenson, N. *Young Teachers and Reluctant Learners* (Penguin, 1971)

Hargreaves, D. H. *Social Relations in a Secondary School* (Routledge and Kegan Paul, 1967)

Holt, John. *How Children Fail* (1969)

Hoyle, Eric. *The Role of the Teacher* (Routledge and Kegan Paul, 1969)

Jackson, B. and Marsden, D. *Education and the Working Class* (Routledge and Kegan Paul, 1962)

Kemble, Bruce. *Give Your Child a Chance* (W. H. Allen and Pan, 1970)

Lamb, G. L. *Questions Answered about Teaching* (Jordan & Sons, 1949)

Morrison, A. and McIntyre, D. *Teachers and Teaching* (Penguin, 1969)

Neill, A. S. *Summerhill* (Gollancz and Penguin, 1962)

Otty, Nicholas. *Learner Teacher* (Penguin, 1972)

Pedley, Robin. *The Comprehensive School* (Penguin, 1966)

Tropp, Asher. *The School Teachers* (Heinemann, 1957)

Turner, Barry (ed). *Discipline in Schools* (Ward Lock Educational, 1973)

Watkins, Roger (ed). *In-Service Training: Structure and Content* (Ward Lock Educational, 1973)

# Index